The Internet and Problem-Based Learning

Developing Solutions through the Web

William J. Stepien, Peter R. Senn, and William C. Stepien

Zephyr Press

Tucson, Arizona

The Internet and Problem-Based Learning
Developing Solutions through the Web

Grades 6–12

© 2000 by Zephyr Press

Printed in the United States of America

ISBN 1-56976-108-6

Editors: Bonnie Lewis and Jenny Flynn
Illustrations: Julie Freeney
Cover design: Daniel Miedaner
Design and production: Daniel Miedaner

Zephyr Press
P.O. Box 66006
Tucson, AZ 85728-6006
800-232-2187
www.zephyrpress.com
www.i-home-school.com

Library of Congress Cataloging-in-Publication Data

Stepien, William, J., 1943-
    The internet and problem-based learning : developing solutions through the Web /
  William J. Stepien, Peter R. Senn, William C. Stepien.
       p. cm.
    Includes bibliographical references.
    ISBN 1-56976-108-6 (alk. paper)
    1. Internet (Computer network) in education—Problems, exercises, etc. 2.
  Problem-based learning. I. Senn, Peter R. II. Stepien, William, C., 1968- III. Title.

  LB 1044.87 .S84 2000
  371.33'44678—dc21

                                                        99-056090

Contents

Preface

The Internet poses a whole new set of challenges and opportunities for the teaching profession. There are still relatively few works available to help the teacher use the Internet. It is our view that the Internet can be a valuable resource for teaching problem solving, one of the most rapidly growing subjects applicable to all curriculums.

This book provides teachers with the materials they will need to introduce their students to the role of the Internet in problem solving. The purpose of the activities is to have students, grades 6 through 12, simultaneously explore significant subject matter content while pursuing a real-world apprenticeship in problem solving.

Many people have helped us create this book. We want to thank everyone at Zephyr Press for making us feel like family, especially Veronica Durie and Jenny Flynn. They knew when to listen, when to suggest, when to soothe, and when to nudge. Anita Lauterstein provided superior secretarial help to Peter. Shelagh Gallagher always knew precisely when Bill Sr. needed advice or an extra dose of writing time. She learned plenty about building with blocks from son Colin during those hours. Kim Stepien gave birth to Justin during manuscript preparation. Love has eternally been an inspiration for writers.

The Internet has the potential to open new worlds for our students. What a shame if they don't recognize those worlds when they enter them. What a handicap if our students don't have the tools to navigate this exciting new frontier.

William J. Stepien
Peter R. Senn
William C. Stepien

Introduction

Who Should Read This Book?

This book is intended for a wide range of teachers, from newly initiated Internet users to those who consider themselves veteran navigators. Its purpose is to provide middle- and high-school teachers with short instructional units (five class periods) that give students practice in locating, evaluating, and thinking with information located on the World Wide Web.

The searching and thinking competencies developed in each unit are like those traditionally used with print materials. However, the very nature of the Internet, with its vast array of sites, presents the opportunity to publish almost anything that comes to mind. This places a special responsibility on schools to be sure that all future problem solvers learn to work responsibly with electronically stored data.

Each instructional unit in this book engages students with standard course content, along with practice in the effective use of Web resources. The authors recognize the pressure on teachers to "cover" the content outlined in their curriculum guides. With this in mind, each problem-solving unit is anchored in typical course content.

The problems in this book will not be easy for students to resolve. They are ill-structured problems, complex and multi-faceted. Each is likely to produce more than one right answer. Students will be required to use reason, not the mechanical application of a formula, to find their way to appropriate solutions. Each week-long problem-solving unit provides students with an authentic apprenticeship in real-world problem solving.

The instructional units also offer teachers a choice of problems to use with their students. The problems highlight content from different disciplines—the natural sciences, language arts, mathematics, social sciences, and fine arts. Teachers might select a unit because it fits nicely into a discipline-specific course. Or, a unit might be selected because of its potential for interdisciplinary study.

What Will This Book Do for You?

This book will show you and your students how to use the Internet to gain a better understanding of a problem, and then come up with solutions likely to produce desirable consequences. Becoming comfortable yourself with the Internet is the first step to making

> The authors recognize the pressure on teachers to "cover" the content outlined in their curriculum guides. With this in mind, each problem-solving unit is anchored in typical course content.

your students comfortable with it. Once that happens, the door is open to a new world of learning.

The problems in the second part of this book have been designed to fit comfortably into the standard curriculum in many courses. This will make it easier for you to infuse Web-based competencies into your curriculum. Appendix III (page 179) of this book is devoted to explaining how to design additional problem-solving units around content you select.

Teaching Goals

This book will help teachers fulfill three important goals. The first is to teach students how to use a computer to access the Internet. The second is to make students comfortable and skillful using the Internet to locate the information needed to help resolve a problem. The third goal is to have students experience problem solving as it is found in the real world—full of challenges, hard work, and opportunities to use their reasoning skills.

What Can the Internet Do for You and Your Students?

The value of the Internet for problem solving lies primarily in its access to information resources and collections of data available in no other way. But information gathering, in itself, is not problem solving, nor is it the equivalent of gaining new knowledge.

On the other hand, knowledge is based on information. All information, especially that found on the Internet, must be rigorously evaluated before the problem solver can trust it enough to build insights and conclusions. The problems in this book show how to organize and evaluate information into a worthy foundation for the support of reasoning.

A Beginning Caution

The Internet is an open system. Pornography and hate literature are easily accessible. Extremists of all kinds propagandize. There is no control over the quality of posted material. The authors suggest that the teacher pay close attention to where students wander while navigating the Web.

The Internet is a new teaching and learning medium. Student assignments should not just be electronic versions of paper-based exercises. Instead, assignments must make effective use of the strengths of the Internet, with its wealth of diverse, timely, and hyper-linked information. Be sure students are encouraged to explore links, to dig deeper, using this powerful tool.

> Student assignments should not just be electronic versions of paper-based exercises. Instead, assignments must make effective use of the strengths of the Internet, with its wealth of diverse, timely, and hyper-linked information.

This book has been designed to be equally beneficial to teachers who are comfortable with computers and the Internet, as well as for the novice user. If you are among the latter, you will find introductory and comprehensive discussions about computers, the Internet, search engines, computer etiquette, and a complete glossary of terms located in the Appendices at the end of this book. An appendix to help you develop your own Problem-Based Learning units is also included. Even the most Web-savvy teachers will find these resources valuable.

Part I

Using the Internet for Problem Solving

Chapter 1

Using the Internet in the Classroom

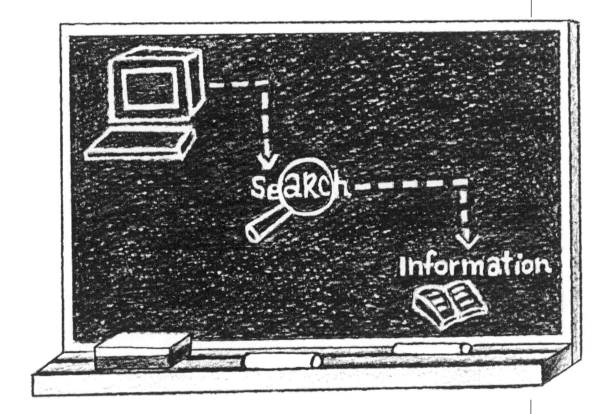

The Internet as an Instructional Tool

Using the Internet for problem solving introduces new dimensions to teaching. New tools—computers and modems—are required to reach the Internet and access the varied resources found there. Using these new tools requires the development of new skills on the part of both the teacher and the students.

Integrating the computer effectively into instruction requires developing skills for making productive use of available computers, even when the number or location of the machines is less than optimal. Organization of time, planning for computer use, and student readiness to use the machines and the Internet must be carefully considered when fusing the Internet with the traditional curriculum.

Organization of time, planning for computer use, and student readiness to use the machines and the Internet must be carefully considered when fusing the Internet with the traditional curriculum.

Using Internet resources for problem solving presents another dimension that needs careful consideration. A teacher must bring actual problems into the curriculum so students need Internet resources to deepen their understanding of the issues. The ill-structured problems you will encounter in this book will provide good practice for improving problem-solving skills, while helping students reach important subject-matter objectives.

Teachers as Coaches

Suppose we are basketball coaches at the opening of a new season. Our players enter the gym and we send them to the bleachers with their notepads and pencils. For the next three hours of practice we lecture on the fine points of the game, show videos of great players, and demonstrate skills. We then quiz them on a few of the hundred plays we will be using this season. How will the team perform in games when the season opens?

Unless the other teams are coached just like ours, we will get creamed! Why? We never invited the players down from the bleachers to "practice" their skills, try out the plays, and learn to work as a team. We can tell them about the game but their performance will not improve until we fade to the sidelines and give them the ball. But we can't leave the gym. A coach watches, supports, corrects, demonstrates, and manages, but the players must practice.

This metaphor is directly applicable to becoming a better performer with computers, the Internet, and problem solving. The players, our students, will improve little if they stay in the bleachers. They will require opportunities to practice on the machines and the Internet. Our students must join us in the practice to experience both successes and failures if they are to perform better in the "game of life." What might appear to be inefficient use of time in the early stages of computer performance will probably pay dividends in the learning process as practice time is accumulated. But don't forget to organize good practices.

Setting Up Classes

Schools differ widely in the access to computers they offer students. Many classrooms are equipped with a single computer. Virtually none have one computer for each student. The most common situation groups computers into one space, a computer laboratory (lab), where computers can accommodate an entire class of about thirty students. Regardless of the number and arrangement of the machines, the first issue a teacher faces in using the Internet is time. How much time on the computer will be available for each student?

> Regardless of the number and arrangement of the machines, the first issue a teacher faces in using the Internet is time. How much time on the computer will be available for each student?

Serious work on the Internet requires that all students have adequate time to use computers. If one or two students at a computer is not possible, form small groups to work with the available machines. As many as three students can work effectively with one computer. Assign students specific tasks during the lesson, and rotate the tasks regularly.

For example, a three-student team's tasks could be divided into: 1) managing the keyboard; 2) recording important information; and 3) managing the search, tracking links to return to, or new ideas to pursue when the current focus runs its course.

When only one computer is available in the classroom, it should be used as a learning station through which small groups of students rotate as a class period unfolds. Using the computer as a learning station requires that alternative stations or tasks be available. A classroom with a limited number of computers but reasonable access to printed materials (such as a media center or in-class library) presents opportunities for comparisons and synthesis of information.

Grouping students has some advantages. It is a good way to cope with differences in student abilities and experiences with computers. Students with computer experience make especially good coaches for those with limited skills. There is a good chance that several students in the class have extensive experience with the Internet. These students should be mentors to novices. They can float from group to group. If there are enough experienced users in the class, each can be assigned to a small group of novices.

Homework on the Computer

On the average, about one-third of all students have access to computers at home. Before starting the problems in this book, identify those students. Check on the availability of computers in your school that can be accessed before school, after school, or during open periods. Finally, the status of computer access at the community library should be determined.

Unless everyone in the class can have fairly easy access to computers outside of class, it will be difficult to assign Internet searches as required homework. But, additional credit can coax students to locate computers in the community to continue their searches outside of the school day. Be sure to have these students share information they find with the entire class through briefing notes or discussion.

When only one computer is available in the classroom, it should be used as a learning station through which small groups of students rotate as a class period unfolds. Using the computer as a learning station requires that alternative stations or tasks be available.

Preparing for the Computer Experience

Computer time is frequently at a premium in schools, so it is usually a good idea to schedule access to available computers well in advance. Before you take your class into the computer laboratory there are several things you must check.

1. **Saving to disk**: Does each machine accept a floppy disk? It is often very useful for the students to save materials on a floppy disk. Find out how your school handles floppy disk distribution. Arrange to get one for each student. Some schools have students save their materials on the computer's hard drive. You must learn, and then teach the students, how to save and access what they have saved.

2. **Printing**: It is sometimes necessary to print the results of an Internet search. You must learn, and then teach the students, how to print material. A word of caution here: access to printing often provokes an avalanche of printing activity. Sources are printed without being evaluated as to their usefulness. Long backups form at the printer, and valuable articles may never get printed because the wait is too long. Students should be taught to evaluate the content of a source before wasting time and paper by printing. If an article contains a small amount of helpful information, it should be recorded on note paper, or saved to a floppy disk. This can be printed out when printer demand has subsided.

3. **Learn how students must sign on to the Internet.** Passwords are almost always required. Make arrangements for student passwords, or learn the steps by which students access the Internet, before taking your class to the computer lab.

Lesson Preparation

The teacher must actually do a lesson before introducing the students to it. Most schools have a person in charge of the computer laboratory. This person will be able to provide much help as the teacher attempts the lesson on his or her own.

The teacher should check the availability of each of the Web sites listed in the students' materials before opening any of the Problem-Based Learning units. Confirming Web sites is mandatory, because they frequently appear and disappear from the Web. If a site has disappeared, or you want to substitute a site more appropriate for your students, suggestions for finding new sites are provided starting on page 28.

A word of caution here: access to printing often provokes an avalanche of printing activity. Sources are printed without being evaluated as to their usefulness.

Evaluating Student Progress

Without adequate evaluation it is impossible to distinguish progress from change. Evaluation of the results of computer use is especially important for many reasons. First, computers are very expensive. Unless they are more than just a fad or classroom decoration, using them should provide results that are measurable. Secondly, computers are a great consumer of students' time. Unless it can be shown that time spent on the computer produces more and better learning than time spent doing other things, why use computers? After all, time is the most valuable resource that students and teachers have.

Each of the problems in this book has procedures for student evaluation. Evaluation takes the form of activities that together form a problem-solving portfolio, called a problem log. Since the problems in this book are authentic representations of real-world problems, the student evaluation activities have been styled to resemble authentic activities likely to be used by actual problem solvers. Therefore, no multiple choice or similar tests are included in the problem logs.

For an introductory explanation of computers and the Internet, read Appendix I (page 169) of this book.

Evaluation takes the form of activities that together form a problem-solving portfolio, called a problem log.

*Chapter 2*_____

Computer Competencies and the Internet

Once the computer is mastered, the Internet can be reached and probed through another powerful tool, the search engine (or browser).

Computer Competencies

In order for students to use the Internet for problem solving, they must have a minimum set of competencies in both the use of the computer and the information uncovered during their Internet searches. The first set of competencies involves manipulating the computer's keyboard and software. Once the computer is mastered, the Internet can be reached and probed through another powerful tool, the search engine (or browser).

Basic Computer Skills Required

Before students can work on the Internet they must have certain skills for using the computer as a tool. The student needs to be able to:

- Turn the computer on and off
- Log on to the computer
- Use a search engine
- Save and delete files on a disk
- Print files
- Understand the following terms: icons, files, bookmarks, links, and menu bar (see the *Glossary of Internet Terms* at end of this book)
- Use the mouse—distinguish between clicking (which highlights an item) and double-clicking (which causes an action)

To be sure your students are acquainted with these skills and terms, test their competence before beginning the problems in this book. Demonstrations with a single computer in the classroom can bring novice users up to speed quickly. If a significant number of students require review, it is a good idea to schedule a session in the computer lab to get everyone comfortable with the machines.

Basic Internet Search Skills Required

Once the students have mastered elementary computer competencies, they are ready to tackle search skills related to the Internet. The students must be able to:

- Launch a search engine
- Access a URL (an address on the World Wide Web) directly or with a bookmark
- Identify and use links

Once able to do these things, students should be able to execute a URL provided by the teacher. Then they should be able to navigate through that site, including its links to similar sites, returning to the starting point when they have finished. When they can do these things, they will be ready to execute a keyword or phrase search on a topic using a specified search engine.

As skills sharpen, the students should be able to perform an Internet search on a specialized topic with different search engines, then compare and contrast the results from these different sources. As they learn more, the students should be able to perform an Internet search with Boolean operators (for more information see page 178), identify reliable sources of online information, and conduct online searches independently. Finally, they should be able to

Demonstrations with a single computer in the classroom can bring novice users up to speed quickly. If a significant number of students require review, it is a good idea to schedule a session in the computer lab to get everyone comfortable with the machines.

download text files to their word-processing software. The more advanced students should learn to download graphics, sound, and video files.

Search Engines— the Key to Finding What You Want

When you use the Internet for problem solving you will be looking for information of various types. This may include data about problems, solutions that are proposed for them, opinions about them, and laws or regulations that apply. The good news is that most of the information you want is out there. The bad news is that it is sometimes hard to find simply because there is so much information on the Internet.

To access the Internet for problem solving you will need to be able to use a search engine. But which one? There are hundreds. And, to complicate things, different search engines do searches in different ways. If a search engine is not used carefully it will return far too many results—or none at all.

Because there is no standard classification of information items on the Internet, search engines are not interchangeable. For example, two favorites, Yahoo *(www.yahoo.com)* and AltaVista *(www.altavista.com)*, are organized on different principles. Yahoo is organized by subject. AltaVista reads and indexes every word of every file it finds on the Web. AskJeeves For Kids *(www.ajkids.com)* is organized around answering questions you ask it. AskJeeves tries to lead you to a Web page that provides an answer. If AskJeeves cannot answer a question, it tries to find a search engine that can. It is one of the few search engines that eliminate references to material inappropriate for children.

No single search engine does a completely satisfactory job for all potential uses. It has been estimated that even the best search engine will only find about 20 percent of the available material on a topic during its search of the Internet.

For a detailed explanation on how search engines work, how to do a search with different types of browsers, and tips for successful searches, see Appendix II (page 175) at the end of this book.

Search Engines for the Challenged User

The majority of material on the Internet is designed on the assumption that everyone has excellent vision and is free of learning disorders. However, two search engines, or browsers, can be helpful to those who are challenged learners.

> The good news is that most of the information you want is out there. The bad news is that it is sometimes hard to find simply because there is so much information on the Internet.

The Lynx *(www.home.unix-ag.org/sfx/lynxit.html)* has the capability to show only the text on a Web page. As a result, its screens are not cluttered with graphics. Some experts call it the browser-of-choice for users who find glitzy Web sites annoying or distracting.

Another browser, pwWebSpeak *(www.prodworks.com/productsindex.htm)*, was designed for users who are visually impaired. It uses large text and presents information by way of spoken language. This format may also benefit students with dyslexia or other leaning disabilities, as well as those learning new languages.

Using Information from Searches

In order to use effectively information uncovered in searches, students need to understand how it fits into a whole. This means the students must develop the ability to:

- Identify issues in a problem
- Recognize when information is needed to better understand the issues
- Conduct successful searches for that information
- Organize the results of the searches
- Evaluate and uncover information for its relevance and reliability
- Then use reliable information to build new insights into the issues in the problem

The eight Problem-Based Learning units in this book provide needed practice with these skills. By conducting successful searches on the Internet, and then using what they find productively, students become more competent seekers and users of information.

The majority of material on the Internet is designed on the assumption that everyone has excellent vision and is free of learning disorders. However, two search engines, or browsers, can be helpful to those who are challenged learners.

Chapter 3

The Nature of Problem-Based Learning

Problem Solving in the Classroom

Most teachers have an interest in helping students become effective problem solvers. Few schools give explicit attention to this skill, however, even though it regularly appears in their mission statements and curriculum guides. If problems are considered at all, they are typically encountered as tidy activities at the end of a unit, and function more as quizzes than opportunities to refine problem-solving skills. Moreover, text-based problems often present students with sterile heuristics. Frequently, these mechanical models are considered more important than the problems they are meant to help solve.

The instructional materials in this book are designed as Problem-Based Learning units. They present significant subject matter content, while providing students with an apprenticeship in real-world problem solving. Each unit features the Internet as the principle medium for gathering information. The Internet is to be searched for information that brings the students to a deeper understanding of the issues in each problem.

Problems That Teach

In Problem-Based Learning, students encounter challenging situations with undefined problems, incomplete information, and unasked questions at the opening of a unit. The scenarios presented to students demand problem solving the way it exists in life. This requires: identifying and detailing issues; creating hypotheses; conducting investigations; developing solutions that fit criteria; and evaluating and justifying potential solutions.

In the process, students criss-cross domains of knowledge, making interdisciplinary connections. They move forward, hit dead ends, revisit data and ideas, revise their thinking, choose new paths, and move on. They will build substantial knowledge bases, enter into real collaborations with classmates, and learn to solve problems— instead of just hearing about problem solving. In the process, students become decidedly different learners.

Problem-Based Learning requires redesign of curriculum and instruction, based upon the observations of expert problem solvers. The first observation involves the size and nature of the knowledge base experts bring to their work. Productive problem solvers possess extensive understanding regarding the issues they are working on. Much of that knowledge is constructed while solving problems. They also know how to find new information when they are puzzled, confused, or at a roadblock in their thinking.

In Problem-Based Learning, information is the raw material for thinking and the construction of new knowledge. The eight problems in this book begin with situations involving ill-structured problems. Resolution of the problems requires that students search for new information, in this case on the Internet, and build their knowledge base through investigation and inquiry.

Imagine, metaphorically, an extensive knowledge base as one blade of a pair of scissors. The scissors represent a tool that can be used to better understand a problem, then find appropriate solutions. But knowledge accounts for only one blade of the scissors. Another blade must be added to make the tool complete.

That second blade is experience. The experience that makes novice problem solvers more skilled involves opportunities to use

The instructional materials in this book are designed as Problem-Based Learning units. They present significant subject matter content, while providing students with an apprenticeship in real-world problem solving.

The eight problems in this book begin with situations involving ill-structured problems. Resolution of the problems requires that students search for new information, in this case on the Internet, and build their knowledge base through investigation and inquiry.

sound reasoning at the core of real inquiries. This results in experts who are able to recognize problematic situations, form reasonable hypotheses, ask insightful questions, conduct fruitful information searches, think critically, and find appropriate solutions, even when problems contain conflicting ethical appeals.

Expert problem solvers seem to possess a custom-built thinker's tool kit. These tools are acquired through practice and experience in solving real problems, often with guidance from mentors and coaches. In Problem-Based Learning, teachers become cognitive coaches for their students: modeling the use of problem-solving skills, holding students accountable to standards for productive thinking, and then fading toward the sidelines so students become more and more responsible for their own performance.

Problem-Based Learning remodels learning by starting at the tip of an iceberg and taking students on an in-depth journey into its core.

The Iceberg Curriculum

Redesigning aspects of our curriculum around ill-structured problems is especially important in light of the unfortunate trend that is adding new icebergs to our curriculum. What's an iceberg? It's an idea, theme, topic, or skill.

Imagine an ocean filled with icebergs. The ocean is the time we have each year to help our students develop deeper understanding of the content we teach. Our units and courses are overflowing with icebergs—and we keep adding new icebergs all the time.

Packing courses with icebergs means we only have time to teach about the very tip of each. Instead of exploring topics by digging down into their cores—to examine their complexities and their connections to other icebergs—our coverage results in students retaining only minuscule amounts of what they hear. They then are unable to transfer knowledge to new situations, being uninspired by the educational enterprise. The cult of coverage has helped create a curriculum that is "a mile wide and an inch deep." This thin layer of substance is not conducive to developing higher-order thinkers and expert problem solvers.

Problem-Based Learning remodels learning by starting at the tip of an iceberg and taking students on an in-depth journey into its core. It promotes explorations into neighboring icebergs for information that relates to the problem under investigation. The effect of using problems to teach is a revitalized curriculum. It features a reasonable number of problem-solving apprenticeships that simultaneously build the knowledge base of students, while providing them with experience in solving real-world problems. This is all accomplished under the careful guidance of teachers acting as cognitive coaches.

The Ill-Structured Problem

Each Problem-Based Learning unit begins with students encountering an ill-structured problem. Meeting the problem precedes all other activity in a unit. The problem provides an authentic context for learning, and engages students because of its challenge, missing details, and complexity.

Ill-structured problems, like real-world problems:

- Are messy and incapable of being fully understood when first encountered
- Often change their nature as more is discovered about them
- Defy solution by simple formula
- Require careful consideration of the fit between solution and problem
- Illustrate the difficulty of being sure one has "the right answer," because data can be missing or in conflict, even after exhaustive investigation

About Reasoning

The experience needed by students to become better problem solvers involves practice with reasoning in the form of the "scientific method" or "rational inquiry." The inquiry process begins when the problem solver senses or observes a situation that needs to be changed or resolved through reflective thinking, not simple reflexive behavior. The inquiry process continues as major issues and hypotheses are identified. Then questions are formulated that will lead the investigator to relevant, reliable information about the issues. The new information is organized and applied to the issues, using the skills of critical thinking. Finally, the problem solver evaluates the initial hypotheses and decides if another cycle of reasoning is needed. Thinking is recycled until the problem solver is satisfied that he or she knows enough to diagnose or define the problem.

Armed with a definition, the problem solver can begin thinking about possible solutions. The consideration of solutions launches the problem solver into the inquiry process again. The objective this time is to assemble possible solutions to the problem, evaluate each according to explicit criteria, and then select the one that best fits the problem.

It should be obvious that reasoning is not the simple application of a formula. Competence is acquired through using the process repeatedly, with a variety of problems and problem variations. As experience accumulates, along with simultaneous growth in knowledge, the problem solver moves from novice status toward that of expert.

> It should be obvious that reasoning is not the simple application of a formula. Competence is acquired through using the process repeatedly, with a variety of problems and problem variations. As experience accumulates, along with simultaneous growth in knowledge, the problem solver moves from novice status toward that of expert.

The Cognitive Coach

Little evidence suggests that students progress toward expert status as problem solvers by merely watching others solve problems. In order to become skillful, they must work firsthand at solving problems. Putting students at the center of the problem-solving process requires that teachers take on a new role. They become their students' cognitive coaches during Problem-Based Learning.

An effective cognitive coach recognizes the relationship between practice and performance. It is when students are actually problem solving that the coach can observe, diagnose, facilitate, and model behaviors most likely to improve performance. Without putting students "in the game" of problem solving, they have little opportunity to improve their performance.

Cognitive coaches are responsible for:

- Adjusting challenges during inquiry so students remain attentive and engaged
- Fostering metacognition by guiding students through reflections on their performance
- Supporting intellectual risk taking and self-directed learning
- Modeling exemplary inquiry skills
- Nurturing skill in interpersonal relations

The instructional units in this book are designed to bring Problem-Based Learning into middle- and high-school classrooms in ways that support student achievement of standard curricular outcomes. Additionally, the problems put students at the center of the inquiry process, doing the work of real problem solvers, using the Internet as a primary source of information.

Phases of Each Problem-Based Learning Unit

Problem-Based Learning takes students through four distinctive phases of activity during a unit. In order of their appearance, the phases are engagement, inquiry/investigation, resolution, and debriefing.

Problem-Based Learning begins with engagement of the learners. Engagement involves the first one or two sessions of the unit. Students meet their problem, begin to identify issues and hypotheses, and then select questions to guide their inquiry. The engagement portion of the unit builds a blueprint for the next phase.

In the inquiry/investigation phase, students use the key questions identified during engagement to help them gather information and better understand the issues in the problem. They visit information sources, including mentors in the community, if available, determine the relevance and reliability of the information they come in contact

---

Putting students at the center of the problem-solving process requires that teachers take on a new role. They become their students' cognitive coaches during Problem-Based Learning.

Students meet their problem, begin to identify issues and hypotheses, and then select questions to guide their inquiry. The engagement portion of the unit builds a blueprint for the next phase.

with, and organize it in preparation for analysis and eventual synthesis into new knowledge about the issues. Coaches may deliver short episodes of direct instruction during the inquiry to help students with especially complex ideas or skills. Student inquiries often involve iterations of the reasoning process, demonstrating the persistence needed during real problem solving. The inquiry phase of the unit usually concludes with formation of a problem definition or description.

Defining a problem in Problem-Based Learning is more complex than in text-based problem solving. The Problem-Based Learning definition has two important components. First, it identifies the central concern that needs resolution. This might be as straightforward as the central concern in the poetry problem (page 73) in this book. As poets, the students must create a poem that can be displayed on the Web site of William Carlos Williams. But in reality the problem is deeper and more complex than that. A complete definition requires the identification of criteria that will separate acceptable, appropriate solutions from all others.

After digging deeply into the life of Williams, and the impact his work has had on other poets, students should identify criteria for an appropriate poem to introduce his home page. The criteria might include:

1. Using a poetic form reflective of Williams' style
2. Using topics similar to those featured in Williams' poems, such as urban life and the "common" person

Now the problem has been defined with more precision, and criteria are in place to judge the appropriateness of solutions. Ill-structured problems often come with a range of possible solutions. But not every solution is appropriate. Therefore, criteria must be produced to help the problem solver decide which is the most fitting choice from the range of possibilities.

The third phase of the unit is the consideration of solutions. In this phase, students need to re-enter the inquiry process to construct solution alternatives. They may run across new issues, and need to assemble additional information. Certainly the students will need to identify positive and negative consequences of potential solutions, then select those likely to be effective and ethical.

The final phase of a Problem-Based Learning unit calls for debriefing student performance. After students prepare their solution products, they retrace problem-solving strategies and extend their insights to contemporary situations. "What if . . ." statements help students transfer what they have learned when a factor in the situation is altered. The coach can review concepts or skills and, if necessary, teach them again. Debriefing is especially important for

> In the inquiry/investigation phase, students use the key questions identified during engagement to help them gather information, and better understand the issues in the problem.

> The third phase of the unit is the consideration of solutions. In this phase, students need to re-enter the inquiry process to construct solution alternatives.

developing the metacognitive insights of the students. The new insights should then be used to improve performance in the next problem-solving situation.

The summative assessment of a student's performance in every Problem-Based Learning unit is the solution product. This is the product developed by each student that presents or communicates a solution, and the rationale for selecting it. It too should be authentic. It should not sound or look like a traditional evaluation assignment.

For example, consider the students acting as lawyers in a scenario involving a parade permit for a hate group (see page 182). They would authentically be expected to send a detailed memo to the mayor or city council with the legal background for the situation and legal rationale for their advice. Authentic assessments coax out so much more information about student thinking than can be found on traditional multiple choice tests.

> The summative assessment of a student's performance in every Problem-Based Learning unit is the solution product. This is the product developed by each student that presents or communicates a solution, and the rationale for selecting it.

Chapter 4

Overview of Problem-Based Learning Units

Collective Coaching Plan

This chapter provides information to help you incorporate the Problem-Based Learning units into your classes. These notes constitute an overview and a collective coaching (or lesson) plan that applies to all of the units. The topics covered here include objectives, sequence of activity in the units, assessment ideas, ideas for extending the units, and a final word of caution about the need to check and update Internet sites you use with your classes. Chapter Five, the next chapter, introduces the specific steps you will use to coach the students through each unit.

The topics covered here include objectives, sequence of activity in the units, assessment ideas, ideas for extending the units, and a final word of caution about the need to check and update Internet sites you use with your classes.

Objectives

The specific subject matter objectives that appear at the beginning of each unit have been adapted from *Content Knowledge: A Compendium of Standards and Benchmarks for K-12 Education* (Kendall and Marzano 1996). The objectives that follow are the inquiry and Internet competency goals common to all eight units.

Inquiry (Problem-solving) Objectives

Students will be able to:

- Identify issues and form hypotheses when they meet an ill-structured problem
- Compile a list of essential questions that need to be answered in order to deepen their understanding of the problem
- Plan and conduct searches for information that answer their essential questions
- Use higher-order thinking to organize and evaluate their collected information
- Evaluate their hypotheses using knowledge constructed from collected information
- Accurately define the problem they need to resolve
- Find effective, ethical solutions to the problem

Internet Competency Objectives

Students will be able to:

- Search the Internet for information on a specific issue or to answer a specific question using more than one search engine
- Use advanced search skills to improve the results of an Internet search
- Assess the relevance and reliability of Internet resources
- Synthesize information from multiple Web sites

Sequence of Activity During a Problem-Based Learning Unit

Each plan follows the same sequence of activity, session to session, as the unit unfolds. The units open with the students meeting their problem. Engagement is followed by inquiry and investigation. Students search for information on the Internet that will deepen their understanding of issues in the problem. They put their newly acquired knowledge to work to define the problem and to identify actions that could help resolve it. Finally, they choose a solution and justify their decision. An opportunity to debrief the experience closes each of the Problem-Based Learning units.

Engagement is followed by inquiry and investigation. Students search for information on the Internet that will deepen their understanding of issues in the problem.

Each unit will take the students through engagement, inquiry and investigation, solution building, and debriefing. The sequence of activity in each of the units is organized for the students in the form of six problem log activity sheets. The six problem logs include:

A. Determining the problem
B. Searching for relevant, reliable information
C. Thinking about the issues
D. A second search of the Internet
E. Building solutions
F. The solution product

Each unit will take the students through engagement, inquiry and investigation, solution building, and debriefing.

Sequence of Activity During a Problem-Based Learning Unit

Opening and Engagement

Leads to

Opening and Engagement. Students, in the role of authentic problem solvers, meet a situation containing an ill-structured problem.

Inquiry and Investigation

Leads to

Investigation and Inquiry. Students search for data and cycle through the reasoning process as they: 1) define their problems and 2) consider appropriate solution(s).

Solution Building

Leads to

Solution Building. Students design ethical solutions likely to produce desired outcomes.

Debriefing

Debriefing. The teacher helps students focus on metacognition and review substantive issues in the problem.

Authentic Student Assessments

Authentic assessments, tasks that relate directly to the problem at hand, are suggested here in place of written examinations because the complexity of thinking used during inquiry is difficult to capture with traditional testing instruments. Besides, few problem solvers face examinations as they are working on a problem.

Authentic assessments also function as excellent learning devices for students. This is because they keep learners in the context of the problem, take the form of "real work," and provide both the learner and the coach with feedback on each student's progress. The problem logs in the units in this book provide many opportunities for authentic assessment, depending on time and preference. Coaches might use the logs to assess student progress, formally or informally, in any of the following ways:

- Assess only Problem Log F, the final solution product
- Assess all log activities individually
- Assess select log activities
- Assess all log activities together in the form of a portfolio
- Use log activities to report student progress in the form of letter grades (see page 33 for help with that)

Using Rubrics to Assess Problem Log Activities

A rubric, or a set of evaluative criteria usually organized as a chart, will help you to assess students' performance on specific activities in the Problem-Based Learning units. Let's explore how you might assess students' performance on Problem Log A, from any of the units in this book. This log asks students, after reading the opening situation, to develop a list of three issues and four questions that will help them better understand the problem. Before the work of developing the lists begins, discuss with the students what would make these short lists effective tools for uncovering information. Explain that you will use important criteria, called a rubric, as a guide to assess the quality of the lists they produce. Develop the rubric with the class or present them with one you have produced in advance. The rubric should follow a model similar to the one on page 25.

This rubric targets the tasks of identifying important issues and constructing questions. It presents criteria for levels of quality developed by the teacher or jointly by the class and the teacher.

Constructing Your Own Rubrics

To construct your rubrics, consider using the general standards for critical thinking found in the *Critical Thinking Handbook: High*

Sample Rubric for Problem Log A

Skill Targets	Performance Level				
	Distinguished	Accomplished	Competent	Ineffective	Not Demonstrated
Identifying Issues— uses a problem's context to find clues pointing to important, relevant issues	Analyzed the situation from many perspectives and found important clues for three significant, relevant issues	Analyzed the situation from more than one perspective and found clues for two significant, relevant issues	Read over situation completely and found clues to at least one important, relevant issue	List of issues was incomplete or made up of insignificant issues	Did not pay attention to the situation; no relevant issues were listed
Constructing Questions— constructs questions that lead to important, relevant information	All four questions were clearly worded; more than one focused sharply on one important, relevant issue	All four questions were clearly worded; one of the questions focused on an important, relevant issues	Three of the questions were clearly worded and likely to lead to some relevant information	One of the four questions was likely to produce relevant information	Four distinctive questions were not produced; questions were unlikely to produce relevant information

School (Paul, Binker, and Adamson 1995). These standards include clarity, precision, accuracy, depth, completeness, relevance, logic, significance, fairness, and consistency. These standards can be adapted to use with the problem log activities in this book. For instance, to construct a rubric to evaluate Problem Log F, you might target the following:

- Depth of understanding of the issues in the problem
- Identification of significant consequences of alternative actions
- Consistency of solution with the definition of the problem
- Clarity of the written communication

Write these targets along the left side of your rubric chart. Then identify how you will identify students' achievement of each of the targeted criteria at the various performance levels (from distinguished to ineffective). Use this information to complete your rubric chart. You'll find that the rubric focuses your assessment, and eliminates debates with students about your "subjectivity."

Extending the Length of the Units

Time for direct instruction during these units is at a premium. However, if time allows, you may want to use the following ideas to help students develop more sophisticated approaches to searching for and using online information to address problems.

Extension 1: Determining a Web Site's Credibility

Before information can be used with confidence, you must know where it comes from and who produced it. The address for a Web site, its uniform resource locator (URL), is the first place to look when deciding how much confidence you can have in the site. URLs begin with a domain name that includes the site's name and category. After the site's name, a code identifies the type of organization that owns the site:

▶ **.com**
identifies profit-making business and organizations

▶ **.edu**
identifies educational institutions

▶ **.gov**
identifies elements of the national government and state agencies

▶ **.int**
identifies international organizations

▶ **.mil**
identifies elements of the United States military

▶ **.net**
identifies groups involved with running the Internet

▶ **.org**
identifies non-profit organizations

▶ **.de**
an example of the two-letter codes used to identify the home country of a Web site (.de identifies Germany)

Evaluating a Web Site with Your Students

When students find a potentially useful site on the Internet, ask them to evaluate its credibility by answering these questions about timeliness, documentation, fact vs. opinion, and author's bias or balance.

1. What kind of site is it? Have students decide if the category of the site makes them more or less confident in it as a source. What is the basis for this impression?

2. What do you know about the Web site's owner? Have students explore a site to find the name of its owner and something about the reasons why the site was created. Is this information available? Is anything mentioned about the owner's background? What can happen to your confidence in a site if it does not include background information about its owner and the purpose for which it was created?

3. Is it credible? When students find a potentially useful site on the Internet, ask them to evaluate its credibility by answering these questions about timeliness, documentation, fact vs. opinion, and author's bias or balance.

- **Timeliness.** When was the information first posted? When was it last updated or revised? Does the timeliness of this information affect its reliability?
- **Documentation.** Is it statistical or a narrative? What is the source of the information? Is it a primary document or a secondary source? Has it already been organized in some way? What do you know about how the information was originally collected?
- **Fact or opinion?** Is the information used to support a point of view? Is information offered that supports other points of view?
- **Author's bias or balance.** If information is offered as fact, what authority is it based upon? If the site has links to other sites, do any of the other sites present another perspective? Does the author use extreme language in presenting information or expressing opinions? Is there balance in the information? Is more than one point of view presented? Was any evidence of bias detected anywhere on this site? What was the evidence? If a site presents a very biased perspective on an issue, can the information still be useful in any way? If the site links to other sites, do any of the other sites present another perspective?

Extension 2: Using Multiple Search Engines

Searching the Internet for relevant, reliable information can be very frustrating. Frequently, more than one search engine will have to be used to ensure enough sites have been searched to find what you are looking for. A thorough discussion of search engines can be found in Appendix II (page 175) of this book. It reviews the various search engines and the methods they use to locate requested information. Students should be encouraged to try different search engines until they find one or two they can use effectively. Additional detailed information about various search engines can be found at *http://searchenginewatch.com*

Extension 3: Using Advanced Search Techniques

Novice Internet users need practice planning their own Internet searches and using multiple search engines. Have the students find the places where their search engines give tips on advanced search techniques. Advanced techniques are those that go beyond simply selecting a search word or phrase that seems appropriate. From the advanced search tips section, have students create a crib sheet for themselves that describes how to use advanced search functions with their search engine. Be sure the crib sheet covers:

> Novice Internet users need practice planning their own Internet searches and using multiple search engines. Have the students find the places where their search engines give tips on advanced search techniques.

- How to search with meaningful phrases, created with the help of quotation marks, in the place of simple words or word groups
- How to include or exclude results from a search using plus (+) and minus (-) signs
- How the Boolean operators AND, AND NOT, and OR (see discussion on Boolean logic in Appendix II on page 178) can narrow or enlarge your list of hits to produce better results
- How to do a wildcard search that recognizes variations of a term
- How to search for a specific URL if you know it

A Final Caution—Updating Internet Sites

The Internet is notorious for leading users to sites that are no longer in operation, have moved to different URLs, or have not been updated in a long time. Furthermore, few Web sites are adjusted for the sophistication of the user. To minimize these problems, check the sites listed in the students' material provided in this book well in advance of opening a unit.

If you wish to substitute Web sites and key terms for those in the students' material, the search phrases used to find the original sites are listed below. They provide a good place to begin a search for substitute sites.

Using the terms **"genetically modified foods"** or **"genetically engineered foods"** with a search engine, click on *websites* or *webpages* to find sites like these:

- British Broadcasting System
  http://news.bbc.co.uk/hi/english/health
  (Use the *Search BBC News Online* box.)

- American Council on Science and Health
  http://www.acsh.org
  (Use the *Search ACSH* feature.)

- Monsanto Company
  http://www.monsanto.com

- Physicians and Scientists for Responsible Application of Science and Technology
  http://www.psrast.org/indexeng.htm

Using the terms **"slavery"** + **"underground railroad"** with a search engine, click on *websites* or *webpages* to find sites like these:

- National Geographic Society
  http://www.nationalgeographic.com/features/99/railroad

- The History Channel
  http://www.historychannel.com/exhibits/undergroundrr/

- University of California at Davis
  http://education.ucdavis.edu/NEW/STC/lesson/socstud/railroad/contents.htm

- Africa Community Watch
  http://www.niica.on.ca/csonan/UnderRailway.htm

Using the term **"William Carlos Williams"** with a search engine, click on *websites* or *webpages* to find sites like these:

- Addison Wesley Longman's Literature Online
  http://occ.awlonline.com/bookbind/pubbooks/kennedy2_awl/chapter18/objectives/deluxe-content.html

- Modern American Poetry
  http://www.english.uiuc.edu/maps/poets/s_z/williams/williams.htm

- The Academy of American Poets
  http://www.poets.org/lit/poet/wcwillia.htm

- Levi Asher's Website, "Literary Kicks"
  http://www.charm.net/~brooklyn/People/WilliamCarlosWilliams.html

Using the terms **"Islamic religion"** + **"mathematics"** with a search engine, click on *websites* or *webpages* to find sites like these:

- Totally Tessellated
  http://library.thinkquest.org/16661/history/uses.html

- Suite101.com, Inc.
  http://www.suite101.com/welcome.cfm/4205

- Islam Questions and Answers
  http://www.islam-qa.com/books/dangershome/english.shtml

- Tessellations, Inc.
  http://www.tessellations.com/index.html

Using the terms **"buying"** + **"computer"** with a search engine, click on *websites* or *webpages* to find sites like these:

- Macworld Pricefinder
  http://www.nextag.com/serv/macbuy/custom/cl/index.html

- Lycos
  http://www.lycos.com/computers

- ZDNet
  http://www.zdnet.com/products

- PC Magazine
  http://www.zdnet.com/pcmag

Using the terms **"Brent Spar"** + **"toxic chemicals"** with a search engine, click on *websites* or *webpages* to find sites like these:

- British Broadcasting Company
  http://news2.thdo.bbc.co.uk/low/english/world/newsid_51000/51360.stm

- Shell Oil
  http://www.shell.com/home
  (Use *search* box.)

- Greenpeace
  http://greenpeace.org/~comms/brent/brent.html

- Environmental Defense Fund
  http://www.scorecard.org/chemical-profiles

Using the terms **"Galileo"** + **"inquisition"** with a search engine, click on *websites* or *webpages* to find sites like these:

- Catholic Encyclopedia
  http://newadvent.org/cathen
  (Type "Galileo" in the *search* box.)

- Rice University
  http://es.rice.edu/ES/humsoc/Galileo/galileo_timeline.html

- Fordham University
  http://www.fordham.edu/halsall/mod/1630galileo.html

- Catholic Educator's Resource Center
  http://catholiceducation.org
  (Use *search* box.)

Using the term **"Rolling Stones"** with a search engine, click on *websites* or *webpages* to find sites like these:

- Rock and Roll Hall of Fame and Museum
  http://rockhall.com/hof/inductee.asp?id=182

- All Music Guide
  http://www.allmusic.com/index.html
  (Use *search* box.)

- Lycos
  http://music.lycos.com
  (Use *search* box.)

- Rolling Stone Magazine
  http://www.rollingstonc.com
  (Click on "R" in "Artists A to Z" and follow links.)

Chapter 5

Coaching Students through Each Problem

Planning for the Unit

Extension Activities

Each of the eight problems in this book are designed to be completed within five 50-minute class sessions. A 10-class-session plan would allow time for a deeper experience with Internet resources and thinking skills. However, the scarcity of time in our curriculum may make even five class periods difficult to find. Thus, these Problem-Based Learning units are a compromise between time pressure and depth of inquiry. The problems can be extended by including skill-building exercises, activities, laboratories, and presentations that might otherwise be offered within a more traditional unit organization.

Using Direct Instruction in Problem-Based Learning

Although it is best when teaching through inquiry to help students to "construct" their own insights as much as possible through the problem-solving process, there are times when they need a little help. Before coaching a unit, identify topics that, given the real time constraints in the classroom, may require you to provide direct instruction to the students.

For instance, while coaching students through Problem-Based Learning Unit 1 (Stop the Frankenfood Monster!), you may wish to prepare them by reviewing the basics of genetics. They may also benefit from a primer on how scientists genetically modify specific foods. During PBL Unit 2 (What Will You and Charles Do?), your class may need to learn about the laws governing slavery during the years preceding the Civil War. Your presentation of PBL Unit 3 (Poetry about Everyday People) may call for a lesson on poetic forms. During PBL Unit 8 (Legends of Rock & Roll), you may even have to introduce your students for the very first time to the music and legacy of the Rolling Stones!

Students often need direct instruction in process as well as content. They will appreciate your assistance as they learn to create workable problem definitions from the messy, "ill-structured" problems they encounter in all the units.

Arriving at Letter Grades

The completed problem log activities provide important and useful information on each student's progress as the unit unfolds. Announce your intention to use the logs for assessment before collecting them. Discuss the criteria that will be used to assess student progress and display them in the classroom. An assessment rubric gives students examples of *distinguished, accomplished, competent, ineffective,* and *not demonstrated* performance levels for each criteria. Letter grades can result from the use of rubrics. Consistent distinguished performance in most of the criteria could be considered "A" work; consistent accomplished performance, "B" work; consistent competent performance, "C" work. Ineffective work or non-production could receive a "D" or "F." See page 24 for more information on rubrics and authentic assessment.

Letter grades can result from the use of rubrics. Consistent distinguished performance in most of the criteria could be considered "A" work; consistent accomplished performance, "B" work; consistent competent performance, "C" work. Ineffective work or non-production could receive a "D" or "F."

Session 1: Engagement

Before the Unit Opens

Before coming to class, have the students read the situation and complete Problem Log A, sections 1 and 2. (Note: Whenever references are made to problem logs, consult any of the eight student problem units for an example.)

In-Class Activity

As a group, use 20 minutes to create a list of issues and questions. This list will be used to open an inquiry into the problem. Before this session ends, decide which questions would be the best to answer first. They will be the focus for Internet searches during the next class session.

Arrange students into small groups. Have each group use 10 minutes to prepare a list of issues and questions members consider important for better understanding the situation. As a whole class, use 20 minutes to create a more refined list of issues and questions. This list will be used to open an inquiry into the problem. Before this session ends, decide which questions would be the best to answer first. They will be the focus for Internet searches during the next class session. **Close the session by organizing small work teams around each question.**

Out-of-Class Assignment

Have students complete Problem Log A, sections 3 and 4. These questions prompt metacognitive reflections to help students think about their own thinking. Students can be asked to volunteer some of their reflections at the opening of the next session or during a debriefing at the close of the unit. Also assign Problem Log B, section 1.

Generalizations

Use the subject matter objectives, found at the start of each unit, as a source of generalizations to be developed during each individual unit.

Learning Resources

- Problem Log A
- Problem Log B
- Computer seating chart. Before beginning work with the Internet, assign each student or work group to a computer. A computer seating chart will save time when the students arrive in the lab for subsequent sessions.
- Substitute Web sites. Check the availability of each the Web sites listed on Problem Log B. If they are unavailable or inappropriate for your students, find substitutes before the class begins. A chart that lists the keywords and phrases, used by the authors to locate the sites listed in the problem

logs, is provided in Chapter 4. The same words and phrases could be used to find alternative sites to those in the students' materials.

Essential Questions

These questions help students construct new knowledge from the information they have gathered and gain insights into their problem-solving behavior.

- What do we know?
- What do we need to know?
- Why do we need to know that?
- How can we find out?
- What might explain that?
- What seem to be the most important issues to understand? Why are they so important?
- What are the most important questions to answer first?

Add questions to the list that will help students probe the situation, clarify their stake in the problem, and identify questions for investigation that will deepen their understanding of important issues in the problem.

Session 2: Inquiry and Investigation

In-Class Activity

Arrange students at computer stations according to your computer seating chart. Call attention to the Web sites listed in section 2 on Problem Log B. These are the sites students will use today to search for information. Links at the sites can be used if time is available.

The students should record relevant information they find on additional sheets of paper, titling each sheet with the site's URL and its owner.

Creating small groups with three students in each differentiates the work at each computer. One student is in charge of the keyboard, one records information, and the third monitors the site for evidence of reliability. Rotate these roles during the class session. At the close of the session, have students summarize what they have discovered by answering sections 4 and 5 on Problem Log B as an out-of-class assignment.

Learning Resources

- Access to computers
- Problem Log B
- Computer seating chart
- Direct instruction, if needed

Creating small groups with three students in each differentiates the work at each computer. One student is in charge of the keyboard, one records information, and the third monitors the site for evidence of reliability.

Essential Questions

- Is the information at this site relevant?
- How can you decide?
- Is it reliable? How can you decide?

If the students explore links:

- What will you be looking for?
- How will you select a link to explore?
- Add your own additional essential questions

Session 3: Inquiry and Investigation (Sharing Session)

In-Class Activity

Review ideas found in Problem Logs A and B. Comment on student insights related to metacognition.

Open a discussion of the information gathered through the Internet search by asking: "What did you find that is important to help us understand our problem?" Fade from the discussion as much as possible, letting the students determine depth and direction. Re-enter the discussion to model good thinking, challenge sloppy thinking, and direct thinking back on course if it strays too far afield. Students should complete section 1 on Problem Log C as the discussion unfolds.

Before the session ends, discuss Problem Log C, section 2 with the students. Sections 2, 3, and 4 will be completed outside of class.

Out-of-Class Activity

Problem Log C, sections 2, 3, and 4

Assessment Suggestions

Any or all of the work done on Problem Log C would provide rich information for assessment.

Learning Resources

- Problem Log C
- Direct instruction (see below)

Direct Instruction

Students will need practice with problem definition. A useful exercise is to have them define everyday problems in the manner called for on Problem Log C. For example, ask them to define the problem they face standing on one side of a busy highway, wanting to get to the other side. Obviously, they need to get to the other side. But that's not all there is to it. Some ways of crossing are better than others. We must consider safety, pedestrian laws, traffic control devices, and the urgency to cross. When these considerations or criteria are used, some solutions become better than others.

Essential Questions

- How did you decide the information was reliable?
- How can we organize our information?
- How does the information help us better understand our problem?
- Did you find facts, opinions, or inferences?
- How do you distinguish between them?
- What evidence do you base that upon?
- Why might views differ on this question?

Session 4: Inquiry and Investigation

In-Class Activity

Review items from yesterday's assessments. If a second Internet search will be conducted, decide if it is to be conducted by individual students or small groups. Be sure each individual or team has a question to investigate and understands the three options in Section 1 of Problem Log D.

Relevant information is to be collected on Problem Log D. An alternative to another computer search might be direct instruction. This alternative can be combined with further discussion of the information from the first computer search and synthesized into generalizations. If only a few students will conduct another search today, they should be ready to add their information to the discussion by the end of the session. If time remains, review the definitions from yesterday and note changes that may have occurred because of today's discussion.

Out-of-Class Activity

Students should complete section 3 on Problem Log D and section 1 on Problem Log E.

Learning Resources

- Problem Log D
- Problem Log E
- Direct instruction, if needed

Essential Questions

Recycle questions from the first Internet search if a second search is conducted. To help students form generalizations, these questions will be helpful:

- What did you find that is important for us to know?
- How can we group or categorize this information?
- What reasonable conclusions can we make?
- How would you sum up what you know so far?
- What new questions have come up?
- What hunches of yours (hypotheses) seem to make sense? Why?
- What new hunches are on your mind?

Session 5: Solution Building and Debriefing

In-Class Activity

Review insights and issues reflected in the metacognitive responses written to this point.

With the large group, brainstorm a list of actions that might help resolve the problem based upon what the students have learned. Discuss possible positive and negative consequences of the options. Students should complete section 2 on Problem Log E while the discussion is taking place.

Out-of-Class Activity

Before beginning Problem Log F, the resolution of the problem and the summative assessment for the unit, have the students discuss section 3 on Problem Log E. Each student will complete Problem Log F out of class. The completed solution product should be treated as the summative assessment for the unit.

Learning Resources

- Problem Log F
- Direct instruction (if needed)

Essential Questions

- How did you arrive at that solution?
- Why do we want that to happen?
- What needs to happen?
- How can that be accomplished?
- Why is that a good solution?
- What are alternative ways of doing that?
- What would be the consequences of that action?
- Considering the consequences, is that action ethical?

Debriefing Activities

Ask students to consider the situation again within a "what if . . ." context. For example: "What if . . . ? Would you change your solution? Why or why not?" Compare the situation itself or its component issues with contemporary situations. Analyze the ethical implications of selected solutions. What ethical appeals support different solutions? Consider, for example, rights, justice, consequences, cost/benefit, and classic virtues. Ask students to consider what they learned about problem solving and their own problem-solving skills.

Part II

Problem-Based Learning Units

Problem-Based Learning Unit 1 ——————————

Stop the Frankenfood Monster!

Unit Synopsis

Students are members of a scientific panel assembled by European governments. Their task is to take an unbiased look into alleged risks associated with using genetically modified and engineered (GM and GE) foods. The problem revolves around a fear that GM foods are dangerous to consumers, and to the natural environment where they are grown.

A Model Definition of the Problem

As a member of the scientific panel, what advice should I give European governments about the alleged risks to human beings from consuming GM foods? What are the possible negative effects on the natural environment from genes that could allegedly escape their intended settings? The advice must consider: 1) the quality of research on the health risks to consumers posed by GM foods; 2) the emotional aspects of the problem; and 3) the technology that produces GM foods.

Subject Matter Objectives

Students will be able to:

- Understand that the variation of organisms within a species increases the likelihood that at least some members of the species will survive under changed environmental conditions.
- Understand that selective breeding for particular traits has resulted in new varieties of cultivated plants and domestic animals.
- Understand that the instructions for specifying the characteristics of the organism are carried in DNA in all organisms.
- Understand that genes are segments of DNA molecules, and that inserting, deleting, or substituting portions of the DNA can alter genes.
- Understand that humans are increasingly modifying ecosystems.
- Understand that new, inheritable characteristics can only result from new combinations of existing genes or from mutations of genes in an organism's sex cells. Other changes in an organism cannot be passed on.
- Understand more about the nature of scientific knowledge and its relationship to scientific inquiry.
- Understand more about the nature of the scientific enterprise and the interactions of science, technology, and society.

Name _____ Date _____ Class Period _____

PBL Unit 1

Stop the Frankenfood Monster!

The Situation

A major battle is brewing between the United
States and a number of European countries. The
controversy is over genetically modified (GM)
foods. The situation threatens to turn millions of
Europeans against American corporations.

In some European countries, political parties
are demanding that their governments halt the
use of all genetically modified food products.
Companies in the United States produce most of
these items.

The concerns of politicians and consumers are
based on research by a British scientist. He claims
that the immune systems of rats have been
severely damaged from eating genetically modified
potatoes. The study comes on the heels of other reports that allergic reactions
almost killed a number of people who ate genetically modified foods.

Protestors at recent demonstrations have enlarged the issue beyond a concern for
human health. They are now carrying signs demanding that governments "Stop the
Frankenfood Monster!" The protestors fear that "monster" genes could escape from
GM plants and destroy the natural environments in their countries.

With protests growing, a plan has been designed to resolve the problem. A
panel of experts will study the situation and then make recommendations on the
future use of genetically modified foods. As one British official explained:
"Someone trustworthy must evaluate the evidence to restore public confidence in
foods, and the government." This is where you come in.

Your Stake in the Problem

You have agreed to join the panel looking into genetically modified foods. The European
governments paying for the panel's work expect an unbiased investigation of the risks GM
foods could pose for consumers and the environment. They want your recommendations
in one week.

Problem Log A—
What Is This Problem About?

1. Issues in the Problem

From what you know so far, list three important issues or elements you think are involved in the problem. These questions can help you think about possible issues.

▶ How did this controversy get started? Why do protestors and consumers fear GM foods? What's the science in the problem? What might be the consequences for consumers and the environment if the protestors are right? What are the consequences if they are wrong?

Issue 1:

Issue 2:

Issue 3:

2. Beginning Your Investigation of the Problem

The panel members need a deeper understanding of the issues in the problem before they can recommend solutions. List four questions your panel should answer in order to get a better understanding of the problem.

Question 1:

Question 2:

Question 3:

Question 4:

3. Thinking about Your Thinking (Metacognition)

Your stake in this problem comes from being a member of a scientific panel. Because of your authority and responsibility as a scientist, what skills and attitudes will you need to bring to the investigation of this problem?

Expert problem solvers frequently examine their own thinking. One thing they want to keep checking on is their own bias. Why is it important to know what biases you bring to the investigation of a problem? What are your personal biases as you approach this problem?

Problem Log B—
Searching for Relevant, Reliable Information

1. Deepening Your Understanding of the Problem

Clearly state the question you want to answer. If the question seems big and complex, break it into smaller questions. Answering the smaller questions might answer the bigger question.

▶ Your question:

▶ Smaller questions:

2. Searching the Internet

The four Web sites below contain information about your problem. They were found by searching the Internet using the keywords or phrases in bold type. Visit one or more of the sites. Collect relevant, reliable information that helps answer your question.

Keywords or phrases: "genetically modified foods" or "genetically engineered foods"

Site 1: http://news.bbc.co.uk/hi/english/health

Site 2: http://www.acsh.org

Site 3: http://www.monsanto.com

Site 4: http://www.psrast.org/indexeng.htm

3. Information from Your First Internet Search

At the top of a sheet of paper, write the three lines found below. Copy the exact URL for the site you are visiting after the line "Internet site." Find the owner of the site, if you can, and add that information after "Owner or controller of the site." Then record relevant information about your question after "Important information." If you visit more than one Internet site, use a separate sheet of paper to record information from each site.

Internet site:

Owner or controller of the site:

Important information:

4. Summarizing What You Learned

After collecting relevant information at a site, summarize what you have learned by answering the question or questions you wrote down at the beginning of your search.

5. Thinking about Your Thinking (Metacognition)

Expert problem solvers make sure the information they use is relevant and reliable. How did you decide if the information you discovered was relevant? How did you decide if it was reliable? What clues at a Web site helped you decide if the information was reliable?

The Internet and Problem-Based Learning, © 2000 Zephyr Press, Tucson, Arizona

Problem Log C—
Thinking about GM Foods

1. Using Information Found by Others

As you discuss what was found on the Internet, record important ideas and how they might be useful in the spaces below. If you are concerned about the relevance or reliability of information being shared, find out where it came from, when it was created, and if any strong bias could be found at the Web site.

▶ Idea:

How might this be useful?

▶ Idea:

How might this be useful?

▶ Idea:

How might this be useful?

2. Defining the Problem

Before trying to solve a problem, it must be defined. What is the problem you need to resolve?

▶ I need to:

I must take into consideration:

1.

2.

▶ Any other factors?

3. Searching for More Information

New information is likely to produce new questions. In the space below, build a new question based on information you have heard so far. Below the question, enter keywords or phrases that are likely to lead you to information that will help you answer the question.

▶ New question:

▶ Keywords and phrases to guide your search:

4. Thinking about Your Thinking (Metacognition)

Problem solving is challenging work. What have you noticed about yourself during this problem regarding each of these characteristics?

▶ Persistence

▶ Precision

▶ Bias

Problem Log D—
A Second Search of the Internet

1. Digging Deeper into the Problem

Information from your first search of the Internet probably helped answer a number of questions about the issues in this problem. New questions have probably come up too. Using the question you wrote for Problem Log C or a brand new question, dig deeper into this problem using one of the options listed below. Report your new findings on another sheet of paper.

▶ Your question:

▶ *Option A:* Look back at the Web sites listed in Problem Log B. If you think there might be information at any of these sites that can help you answer your question, go to that site.

▶ *Option B:* Go back to one of the Web sites listed in Problem Log B. Find links to other Web sites listed on the site you are visiting. Check out one or more of the links by placing the mouse arrow on a link and clicking.

▶ *Option C:* Select a search engine and start a new search of the Web by typing in keywords or phrases you listed in Problem Log C.

2. Information from Your Second Internet Search

Record relevant information found during your search on another sheet of paper. Organize the information under the URLs of the sites you visited.

Internet site:

Owner or controller of the site:

Important information:

3. Thinking about Your Thinking (Metacognition)

It is likely you still do not understand some issues in the problem. But the governments sponsoring the investigation want your recommendations. Experts are often asked to solve problems that have unresolved issues or arguments. What issues or questions about genetically modified foods are still unclear to you? How can the panel make recommendations if some issues still need to be resolved?

Problem Log E— Building Solutions

1. More Than One Solution

It is likely real-world problems can be resolved in more than one way and will require a number of actions before they are completely resolved. Space is provided below for two possible recommendations. For each recommendation, list positive and negative consequences that are likely to result. Use additional paper if necessary.

▶ First recommendation:

Positive consequences:

1.

2.

Negative consequences:

1.

2.

▶ Second recommendation:

Positive consequences:

1.

2.

Negative consequences:

1.

2.

2. Recommendations from Other Members of the Panel

As panel members share their ideas for recommendations, record those that seem like good ideas. Your final recommendations will be collected in a memo addressed to the governments that paid for your services. In that memo, you must be sure to justify or explain why each recommendation is a good or right thing to do. Be sure to give credit in the memo for ideas that came from other panel members. Problem Log F is the blank memo ready for your use.

▶ Recommendation from another panelist:

Positive and negative consequences:

▶ Recommendation from another panelist:

Positive and negative consequences:

▶ Recommendation from another panelist:

Positive and negative consequences:

3. Thinking about Your Thinking (Metacognition)

Before you write your memo, think about what the European governments will be looking for in your work. What do you think they expect as to:

▶ **Clarity:** What will you do to make your work clear and understandable?

▶ **Depth of understanding:** What will you do to show them how well you understand the problem?

▶ **Effectiveness:** What will you do to make sure the situation involving the protestors, governments, and American corporations improves?

Problem Log F—
Memo Describing Final Recommendations

To: Governmental sponsors of the investigation into genetically modified foods

From: _____

Regarding: Recommendations on the use of genetically modified foods

Date: _____

Problem Log F—
Memo Describing Final Recommendations

Continue on additional paper if necessary.

Problem-Based Learning Unit 2

What Will You and Charles Do?

Unit Synopsis

Each student will take on the role of a slave named Joseph, who is living on a Mississippi farm in 1858. Joseph and another slave, Charles, are about to flee for freedom with the help of the Underground Railroad. Charles, Joseph's companion, begins to doubt whether he is making a good decision as they hide by the side of the road waiting for a wagon to pick them up. Charles asks Joseph to go over the details again, to convince him he's making the right choice. Joseph, hearing the doubts Charles expresses, recognizes the same questions in his own mind. As Joseph, the students must decide on a course of action as a wagon appears on the road—presumably a wagon driven by a conductor on the Underground Railroad.

A Model Definition of the Problem

As an enslaved person in 1858 contemplating going north to freedom, what advice will I give my companion to help him decide if he should run away too? My advice must take into consideration: 1) the risks we will encounter along the way; 2) the help that can be given to us by the Underground Railroad; 3) the fate of family members who remain on the farm; and 4) the future we face as runaway slaves in the North.

Subject Matter Objectives

Students will be able to:

- Understand different economic, cultural, and social characteristics of slavery after 1800.
- Understand the social, cultural, and economic influence of fugitive slaves living in the North before the beginning of the Civil War.
- Understand how slavery influenced economic and social elements of Southern society.
- Understand the range of treatment extended toward slaves in the South and to runaway slaves in the North.
- Understand how the Underground Railroad was organized, what methods it used, and how successful it was in achieving freedom for slaves.
- Understand how geography and astronomy played a part in the operations of the Underground Railroad.

PBL Unit 2

What Will You and Charles Do?

The Situation

"Joseph, can we do it?" Charles asks for the third time in ten minutes. "I've got a baby here. Maybe I don't have it so bad? Not as bad as the field slaves. Maybe I should just wait for the war or the Master to die. They say there's going to be a war." The wagon would be coming into sight anytime now. The conductor would be expecting two travelers. You are beginning to suspect there might be just one.

"Charles, we've been through this. You said you wanted to go. You said you wanted to get all the way free, then come back for your family. Why are you backing out now?"

"It's different today, Joseph," Charles begins to explain. "Last month, last week, even yesterday, that was different. Today I'm going to have to climb on that wagon. What if the catchers stop us? What if those Northerners want the reward and send us 'fugitives' back south? Then it's the whip, isn't it, and the collar too. Maybe salt. I don't want any salt on me!"

"Hush, Charles! We'll get caught before we get started with you yelling like that!"

"I need convincing, Joseph. How come you are so sure we can do it?" Charles is starting to shake from fear now.

"I'm not sure, Charles. I just think we can do it, with the help of the railroad. And I think we can do it better together than alone," you say, trying to reassure Charles, and yourself a little too.

The hay wagon comes into sight.

"Explain it to me again! I've got to make up my mind, Joseph. How does this railroad work? How long till I can come back for my family? What do they do with runaways if they catch them? Tell me what I should do, Joseph!"

Your Stake in the Problem

Your name is Joseph. The year is 1858. You live on the Wilbur farm, in the middle of the state of Mississippi. Going north has been on your mind since abolitionists started coming around and talking about freedom, the Underground Railroad, and a place called Canada. But the sight of the wagon is bringing back old fears. Maybe Charles is right? Maybe you can make your life better some other way? How will you explain the situation to Charles? What will you do when the wagon stops?

Problem Log A—
What Is This Problem About?

1. Issues in the Problem

From what you know so far, list three important issues involved in your problem. These questions can help you think about possible issues.

▶ Why did slaves try to escape north? What type of help did they receive? What happened if they were captured and returned? Were there any other ways to gain freedom besides becoming fugitives? What did freedom actually mean for a fugitive slave?

Issue 1:

Issue 2:

Issue 3:

2. Beginning Your Investigation of the Problem

You probably need a deeper understanding of the issues before you can convince Charles, and yourself, of the right thing to do. List four questions you should answer in order to get a better understanding of the problem.

Question 1:

Question 2:

Question 3:

Question 4:

3. Thinking about Your Thinking (Metacognition)

Your stake in this problem comes from being a slave planning your escape to freedom. How does thinking about the problem from a slave's point of view compare with thinking about it as an abolitionist, slave owner, or the student you are, living at the beginning of the 21st century? What will you do to keep the perspective of a slave throughout this problem?

Expert problem solvers frequently examine their own thinking. One thing they want to keep checking on is their own bias. Why is it important to know what biases you bring to the investigation of a problem? What are your personal biases as you approach this problem?

Problem Log B—
Searching for Relevant, Reliable Information

1. Deepening Your Understanding of the Problem

Clearly state the question you want to answer. If the question seems big and complex, break it into smaller questions. Answering the smaller questions might answer the bigger question.

▶ Your question:

▶ Smaller questions:

2. Searching the Internet

The four Web sites below contain information about your problem. They were found by searching the Internet using the keywords or phrase in bold type. Visit one or more of the sites. Collect relevant, reliable information that helps answer your question.

> <u>**Keywords or phrases: "slavery" + "underground railroad"**</u>
>
> **Site 1:** http://www.nationalgeographic.com/features/99/railroad
>
> **Site 2:** http://www.historychannel.com/exhibits/undergroundrr/
>
> **Site 3:** http://education.ucdavis.edu/NEW/STC/lesson/socstud/railroad/contents.htm
>
> **Site 4:** http://www.niica.on.ca/csonan/UnderRailway.htm

3. Information from Your First Internet Search

At the top of a sheet of paper, write the three lines found below. Copy the exact URL for the site you are visiting after the line "Internet site." Find the owner of the site, if you can, and add that information after "Owner or controller of the site." Then record relevant information about your question after "Important information." If you visit more than one Internet site, use a separate sheet of paper to record information from each site.

Internet site:

Owner or controller of the site:

Important information:

4. Summarizing What You Learned

After collecting relevant information at a site, summarize what you have learned by answering the question or questions you wrote down at the beginning of your search.

5. Thinking about Your Thinking (Metacognition)

Expert problem solvers make sure the information they use is relevant and reliable. How did you decide if the information you discovered was relevant? How did you decide if it was reliable? What clues at a Web site helped you decide if the information was reliable?

Problem Log C—
Thinking about Becoming a Fugitive

1. Using Information Found by Others

As you discuss what was found on the Internet, record important ideas in the spaces below. If you are concerned about the relevance or reliability of any of the information, find out where it came from, when it was created, and if any strong bias could be found at the Web site.

▶ Idea:

How might this be useful?

▶ Idea:

How might this be useful?

▶ Idea:

How might this be useful?

2. Defining the Problem

Before trying to solve a problem, it must be defined. What is the problem you and Charles need to resolve?

▶ We need to:

We must consider:

1.

2.

▶ Any other factors?

3. Searching for More Information

New information is likely to produce new questions. In the space below, build a new question based on the information you have heard so far. Below the question, enter keywords or phrases that are likely to lead you to information that will help you answer the question.

▶ New question:

▶ Keywords and phrases to guide your search:

4. Thinking about Your Thinking (Metacognition)

Problem solving is challenging work. What have you noticed about yourself while working on this problem regarding each of these characteristics?

▶ Persistence

▶ Precision

▶ Imagination

The Internet and Problem-Based Learning, © 2000 Zephyr Press, Tucson, Arizona

Problem Log D—
A Second Search on the Internet

1. Digging Deeper into the Problem

Information from your first search of the Internet probably answered a number of questions about issues in the problem. New questions have probably come up too. Using the question you wrote for Problem Log C or a brand new question, dig deeper into this problem using one of the options listed below. Report your new findings on a separate sheet of paper.

▶ Your question:

▶ *Option A:* Look back at the Web sites listed on Problem Log B. If you think there might be information at any of these sites that can help you answer your question, go to that site.

▶ *Option B:* Go back to one of the Web sites listed in Problem Log B. Find links to other Web sites listed at the site you are visiting. Check out one or more of the links by placing the mouse arrow on a link and clicking.

▶ *Option C:* Select a search engine and start a new search of the Web by typing in keywords or phrases that are likely to lead you to sites that will be helpful. For help with selecting key words and phrases, look back at the words listed in Problem Log C.

2. Information from Your Second Internet Search

Record relevant information found during your search on another sheet of paper. Organize the information under the URLs of the sites you visited.

Internet site:

Owner or controller of the site:

Important information:

3. Thinking about Your Thinking (Metacognition)

It is likely you still do not understand some issues in the problem, but you must begin explaining things to Charles soon. Actions are often taken on problems that still contain unresolved issues or arguments. What issues or questions about slavery and the Underground Railroad are still unclear to you? How can you help Charles if these issues have not been cleared up?

The Internet and Problem-Based Learning, © 2000 Zephyr Press, Tucson, Arizona

Problem Log E—
Building Solutions

1. More Than One Solution

Since it is possible for complex, real-world problems to have more than one solution, space is provided on this page to record several ways to help Charles. In the space below, list your suggestions (solutions to the problem) and the positive and negative consequences that are likely to result from each suggestion. Use additional paper if necessary.

▶ First recommendation:

Positive consequences:

1.

2.

Negative consequences:

1.

2.

▶ Second recommendation:

Positive consequences:

1.

2.

Negative consequences:

1.

2.

2. Recommendations from Other Investigators

As other investigators share their recommendations, record those that seem like good ideas. Your final set of recommendations to Charles will be prepared as a dialogue between yourself and your companion. In the dialogue, you must state your recommendations and justify or explain why each action is a good or right thing to do.

▶ Recommendation from other investigator:

   Positive and negative consequences:

▶ Recommendation from other investigator:

   Positive and negative consequences:

▶ Recommendation from other investigator:

   Positive and negative consequences:

3. Thinking about Your Thinking (Metacognition)

Now that your work is finished, think about how well you did your job by answering the questions below. Use additional paper if necessary.

▶ How well did you succeed as a problem solver?

▶ What problem-solving strategies did other students use that impressed you?

▶ The next time you work on a complex problem like this one, what will you do in the same way? What will you do differently?

Problem Log F—
Your Suggestions for Charles

Present your suggestions to Charles as though the two of you are having a conversation. Alternate between yourself and Charles. The three specific questions Charles would like answered are shown below. **Be sure you answer them as a part of the conversation.**

▶ "We're going to get caught, I can feel it! What's going to happen to us if we get caught?"

▶ "How are we going to get from one conductor to the next on the Underground Railroad?"

▶ "I don't want to go to Canada, Joseph. What's wrong with just staying in a Northern state?"

Problem Log F—
Your Suggestions for Charles

Continue on additional paper if necessary.

Problem-Based Learning Unit 3 ———————————

Poetry about Everyday People

Unit Synopsis

Students are poets given an opportunity to create an original poem in honor of William Carlos Williams. Their poems will be showcased on a new Web site celebrating the impact of Williams on modern poetry. The poems should illustrate in some way Williams' choice of subjects for his poetry, and his experimentation with language and poetic forms.

A Model Definition of the Problem

How can I express, in a poem, some aspect of William Carlos Williams' impact on modern poetry? My product must take into consideration Williams' innovative use of language, rule-breaking use of poetic form, and use everyday subjects.

Subject Matter Objectives

Students will be able to:

- Write compositions that clearly fulfill different purposes, including to inform, entertain, and stimulate emotion.
- Understand at an appropriate developmental level the defining features and structure of poems.
- Demonstrate a familiarity with and understanding of selected poems by William Carlos Williams.
- Synthesize information from a variety of sources when researching a topic.

Note: This problem has been designed to unfold over five class periods. No time has been provided for editing and revising the students' poems. The students should be reminded that the poems they are creating are first drafts, that would go through a process of review, revising, and editing a number of times before being considered for publication.

Name _____ Date _____ Class Period _____

PBL Unit 3

Poetry about Everyday People

The Situation

The university has asked you to write an original piece of poetry for the new William Carlos Williams Web site. The school is building the Internet site to celebrate Williams' impact on modern poetry. The project committee wants you to create an original poem to be showcased at the site because you are recognized as an expert in the life and work of the poet. Besides, you are becoming a recognized poet yourself.

The committee hopes your poem will give others insight into the style and ideas of Williams. Unfortunately, space is limited at the site, so you can only use up to ten lines for your work.

Your Stake in the Problem

As a poet just beginning to be widely published, this is a good opportunity to have a spotlight put on your work. More importantly, William Carlos Williams has always been an idol of yours. His choice of subjects, his way of bending the rules, his experiments with language—what's not to admire? Now you have a chance to show your admiration for one of your heroes. It's time to get started—you need a first draft for a short poem in five days. What are you going to write in honor of William Carlos Williams?

Problem Log A—
What Is This Problem About?

1. Issues in the Problem

From what you know so far, list three important issues or elements you think are involved in the problem. These questions can help you think about possible issues.

▶ What does the committee expect? Why have they chosen you? What should be said about William Carlos Williams? What style should be used for the poem? What subjects for the poem would be most appropriate?

Issue 1:

Issue 2:

Issue 3:

2. Beginning Your Investigation of the Problem

You need a deeper understanding of the issues in the problem before you can begin writing a solution—a poem. List four questions you should answer in order to get a better understanding of the problem.

Question 1:

Question 2:

Question 3:

Question 4:

3. Thinking about Your Thinking (Metacognition)

Your stake in this problem comes from being a poet and an admirer of Williams. Because of your authority and responsibility as a poet, what skills and attitudes will you need to bring to the resolution of this problem?

Expert problem solvers frequently examine their own thinking. One thing they want to keep checking on is their own bias. Why is it important to know what biases you bring to the resolution of a problem? What are your personal biases as you approach this problem?

Problem Log B—
Searching for Relevant, Reliable Information

1. Deepening Your Understanding of the Problem

Clearly state the question you want to answer. If the question seems big and complex, break it into smaller questions. Answering the smaller questions might answer the bigger question.

▶   Your question:

▶   Smaller questions:

2. Searching the Internet

The four Web sites below contain information about your problem. They were found by searching the Internet using the keywords or phrases in bold type. Visit one or more of the sites. Collect relevant, reliable information that helps answer your question.

Keywords or phrases: "William Carlos Williams"

Site 1: http://occ.awlonline.com/bookbind/pubbooks/kennedy2_awl/chapter18/objectives/deluxe-content.html

Site 2: http://www.english.uiuc.edu/maps/poets/s_z/williams/williams.htm

Site 3: http://www.poets.org/lit/poet/wcwillia.htm

Site 4: http://www.charm.net/~brooklyn/People/WilliamCarlosWilliams.html

3. Information from Your First Internet Search

At the top of a sheet of paper, write the three lines found below. Copy the exact URL for the site you are visiting after the line "Internet site." Find the owner of the site, if you can, and add that information after "Owner or controller of the site." Then record relevant information about your question after "Important information." If you visit more than one Internet site, use a separate sheet of paper to record information from each site.

Internet site:

Owner or controller of the site:

Important information:

4. Summarizing What You Learned

After collecting relevant information at a site, summarize what you have learned by answering the question or questions you wrote down at the beginning of your search.

5. Thinking about Your Thinking (Metacognition)

Expert problem solvers make sure the information they use is relevant and reliable. How did you decide if the information you discovered was relevant? How did you decide if it was reliable? What clues at a Web site helped you decide if the information was reliable?

Problem Log C—
Thinking about Creating Your Poem

1. Using Information Found by Others

As you discuss what was found on the Internet, record important ideas and how they might be useful in the spaces below. If you are concerned about the relevance or reliability of information being shared, find out where it came from, when it was created, and if any strong bias could be found at the Web site.

▶ Idea:

How might this be useful?

▶ Idea:

How might this be useful?

▶ Idea:

How might this be useful?

2. Defining the Problem

Before trying to solve a problem, it must be defined. What is the problem you need to resolve?

▶ I need to:

My poem must take into consideration:

1.

2.

▶ Any other factors?

3. Searching for More Information

New information is likely to produce new questions. In the space below, build a new question based on information you have heard so far. Below the question, enter keywords or phrases that are likely to lead you to information that will help you answer the question.

▶ New question:

▶ Keywords and phrases to guide your search:

4. Thinking about Your Thinking (Metacognition)

Did you ever think of poets as problem solvers before? What have you noticed about yourself during this problem regarding each of these characteristics?

▶ Persistence

▶ Precision

▶ Creativity

Problem Log D—
A Second Search of the Internet

1. Digging Deeper into the Problem

Information from your first search of the Internet probably helped answer a number of questions about the issues in this problem. New questions have probably come up too. Using the question you wrote for Problem Log C or a brand new question, dig deeper into this problem using one of the options listed below. Report your new findings on another sheet of paper.

▶ Your question:

▶ *Option A:* Look back at the Web sites listed in Problem Log B. If you think there might be information at any of these sites that can help you answer your question, go to that site.

▶ *Option B:* Go back to one of the Web sites listed in Problem Log B. Find links to other Web sites listed on the site you are visiting. Check out one or more of the links by placing the mouse arrow on a link and clicking.

▶ *Option C:* Select a search engine and start a new search of the Web by typing in keywords or phrases you listed in Problem Log C.

2. Information from Your Second Internet Search

Record relevant information found during your search on another sheet of paper. Organize the information under the URLs of the sites you visited.

Internet site:

Owner or controller of the site:

Important information:

3. Thinking about Your Thinking (Metacognition)

It is likely that you still do not understand some issues in the problem. But the committee wants your poem soon. Experts are often asked to solve problems that contain unresolved issues or arguments. What issues or questions about the life, work, and influence of William Carlos Williams are still unclear to you? How can you build a solution, a first draft of a poem for the Web site, if some issues still need to be resolved?

Problem Log E—
Building Solutions

1. More Than One Solution

Since it is possible for complex, real-world problems to have more than one solution, space is provided on this page for a number of ideas about the construction of this poem. List your ideas and the strengths and weaknesses of each. Use additional paper if necessary.

▶ First idea:

Strengths of the idea:

1.

2.

Weaknesses of the idea:

1.

2.

▶ Second idea:

Strengths of the idea:

1.

2.

Weaknesses of the idea:

1.

2.

2. Recommendations from Others

As members of your class share their thinking, record those thoughts that seem like good ideas. Your draft of a poem will be presented to the project committee. In an attachment to your poem, be sure to justify or explain why you created the poem you did. Problem Log F has space for your poem and explanation.

▶ Idea from another poet:

Strengths and weaknesses:

▶ Idea from another poet:

Strengths and weaknesses:

▶ Idea from another poet:

Strengths and weaknesses:

3. Thinking about Your Thinking (Metacognition)

Before you write the first draft of your poem, think about what the project committee will be looking for in your work. What do you think they expect as to:

▶ **Creativity:** How will you tap your creativity for this task?

▶ **Depth of understanding:** How will your work show your understanding of the poetry of William Carlos Williams?

▶ **Appropriateness:** How will your poem make a fitting kickoff for the new Internet site?

Problem Log F—
First Draft

Your poem:

Problem Log F—
First Draft

Author's notes on the elements of the poem:

Continue on additional paper if necessary.

Problem-Based Learning Unit 4 ───────────────

Idolatry in Your Work?

Unit Synopsis

Students are design architects working on the architectural features for the lobby of a significant new building. To blend Moslem culture into decorations for the building's lobby, the students, as architects, have proposed geometric patterns based upon the work of H. C. Escher. The suggestion is widely approved of by the members of the committee, until one of the members points out that Escher's patterns might be a form of idolatry to those practicing the Islamic religion. The students will need to find out what aspects of Escher's work could be labeled idolatrous by the followers of Islam. Then the students must come up with geometric patterns that reflect the rich Moslem traditions in architecture and mathematics, but avoid any possible idolatrous content (representation of human or other animal forms).

A Model Definition of the Problem

As a member of an architectural design team working on a new building, what designs will I submit that: 1) capture the rich traditions of Moslem art, architecture, and mathematics; 2) fit the general motif of the building; and 3) are not idolatrous according to principles of the Islamic religion?

Subject Matter Objectives

Students will be able to:

- Recognize the importance of specific cultural elements in the everyday life of a target culture.
- Understand expressive forms of the target culture.
- Understand that mathematical ideas and concepts can be represented concretely, graphically, and symbolically.
- Perform synthetic and algebraic transformations of basic geometric shapes.

PBL Unit 4

Idolatry in Your Work?

The Situation

From the plans in front of you, it is obvious the building will become a landmark. It has the simple lines of modern architecture, perfectly expressed through concrete, metal, and glass. But somehow the exterior also captures the ageless beauty of Moslem culture, probably through the geometric patterns the surfaces form with one another. A remarkable building!

The people around the conference table come from diverse career fields and ethnicities. Some of them are the actual owners of the building. One member of the group, a businessman from Lebanon who is a major partner in the project, made a comment a few minutes ago that caught you completely off guard. He challenged your ideas for the architectural decoration in the lobby area. You had just mentioned that you were thinking of geometric themes, especially tessellations, worked directly into the materials used for the walls, floors, and ceilings. Then you tossed out an idea about using Escher-like figures as the basis for the patterns. The Moslem businessman was startled by the idea.

"Idolatry. It would be idolatry to do that. You cannot use that idea in our building," he said. Then he leaned forward and added, "The idea of geometric patterns is a wonderful idea, but think about the Islamic religion before you go any further with your design."

At that moment, the man's cellular phone rang. After a brief conversation he offered the group his apology. He needed to leave to take care of a matter that had come up.

Your Stake in the Problem

As the principal design architect on the team, what geometric and artistic patterns will you recommend for the surfaces of the lobby?

The Internet and Problem-Based Learning, © 2000 Zephyr Press, Tucson, Arizona

Problem Log A—
What Is This Problem About?

1. Issues in the Problem

From what you know so far, list three important issues or elements you think are involved in the problem. These questions can help you think about possible issues.

▶   How did this problem get started? Why did the businessman get upset? How is mathematics involved in the problem? How are tessellations produced? What consequences might occur if you don't figure out the problem with your idea?

Issue 1:

Issue 2:

Issue 3:

2. Beginning Your Investigation of the Problem

You need a deeper understanding of the issues in the problem before you can recommend designs for the lobby. List four questions you should answer in order to get a better understanding of the problem.

Question 1:

Question 2:

Question 3:

Question 4:

3. Thinking about Your Thinking (Metacognition)

Your stake in this problem comes from being a part of an architectural design team. Because of your authority and responsibility as a professional, what skills and attitudes will you need to bring to the investigation of this problem?

Expert problem solvers frequently examine their own thinking. One thing they want to keep checking on is their own bias. Why is it important to think about your biases and the perspectives of others as you investigate this problem? What are your own biases as you approach this problem?

Problem Log B—
Searching for Relevant, Reliable Information

1. Deepening Your Understanding of the Problem

Clearly state the question you want to answer. If the question seems big and complex, break it into smaller questions. Answering the smaller questions might answer the bigger question.

▶ Your question:

▶ Smaller questions:

2. Searching the Internet

The four Web sites below contain information about your problem. They were found by searching the Internet using the keywords or phrases in bold type. Visit one or more of the sites. Collect relevant, reliable information that helps answer your question.

Keywords or phrases: "Islamic religion" + "mathematics"

Site 1: http://library.thinkquest.org/16661/history/uses.html

Site 2: http://www.suite101.com/welcome.cfm/4205

Site 3: http://www.islam-qa.com/books/dangershome/english.shtml

Site 4: http://www.tessellations.com/index.html

3. Information from Your First Internet Search

At the top of a sheet of paper, write the three lines found below. Copy the exact URL for the site you are visiting after the line "Internet site." Find the owner of the site, if you can, and add that information after "Owner or controller of the site." Then record relevant information about your question after "Important information." If you visit more than one Internet site, use a separate sheet of paper to record information from each site.

Internet site:

Owner or controller of the site:

Important information:

4. Summarizing What You Learned

After collecting relevant information at a site, summarize what you have learned by answering the question or questions you wrote down at the beginning of your search.

5. Thinking about Your Thinking (Metacognition)

Expert problem solvers make sure the information they use is relevant and reliable. How did you decide if the information you discovered was relevant? How did you decide if it was reliable? What clues at a Web site helped you decide if the information was reliable?

Problem Log C—
Thinking about Possible Designs

1. Using Information Found by Others

As you discuss what was found on the Internet, record important ideas and how they might be useful in the spaces below. If you are concerned about the relevance or reliability of information being shared, find out where it came from, when it was created, and if any strong bias could be found at the Web site.

▶ Idea:

How might this be useful?

▶ Idea:

How might this be useful?

▶ Idea:

How might this be useful?

2. Defining the Problem

Before trying to solve a problem, it must be defined. What is the problem you need to resolve?

▶ I need to:

My design must take into consideration:

1.

2.

▶ Any other factors?

3. Searching for More Information

New information is likely to produce new questions. In the space below, build a new question based on information you have heard so far. Below the question, enter keywords or phrases that are likely to lead you to information that will help you answer the question.

▶ New question:

▶ Keywords and phrases to guide your search:

4. Thinking about Your Thinking (Metacognition)

Problem solving is challenging work. What have you noticed about yourself during this problem regarding each of these characteristics?

▶ Persistence

▶ Precision

▶ Awareness of others' perspectives

Problem Log D—
A Second Search of the Internet

1. Digging Deeper into the Problem

Information from your first search of the Internet probably helped answer a number of questions about the issues in this problem. New questions have probably come up too. Using the question you wrote for Problem Log C or a brand new question, dig deeper into this problem using one of the options listed below. Report your new findings on another sheet of paper.

▶ Your question:

▶ *Option A:* Look back at the Web sites listed in Problem Log B. If you think there might be information at any of these sites that can help you answer your question, go to that site.

▶ *Option B:* Go back to one of the Web sites listed in Problem Log B. Find links to other Web sites listed on the site you are visiting. Check out one or more of the links by placing the mouse arrow on a link and clicking.

▶ *Option C:* Select a search engine and start a new search of the Web by typing in keywords or phrases you listed in Problem Log C.

2. Information from Your Second Internet Search

Record relevant information found during your search on another sheet of paper.
Organize the information under the URLs of the sites you visited.

Internet site:

Owner or controller of the site:

Important information:

3. Thinking about Your Thinking (Metacognition)

It is likely you still do not thoroughly understand some issues in the problem. But the
architectural committee wants your recommendations. Experts are often asked to solve
problems that contain unresolved issues or arguments. What issues or questions about
geometric patterns, architectural design, or the Islamic religion are still unclear to you?
How can you make recommendations if some issues still need to be resolved?

Problem Log E—
Building Solutions

1. More Than One Solution

Since it is possible for complex real-world problems to have more than one solution, space is provided on this page for two design recommendations. Be sure to present both positive and negative consequences that could result from each of your recommendations. Use additional paper if necessary for sketches of the designs you might recommend.

▶ First recommendation:

Positive consequences:

1.

2.

Negative consequences:

1.

2.

▶ Second recommendation:

Positive consequences:

1.

2.

Negative consequences:

1.

2.

2. Recommendations from Other Members of the Committee

As colleagues share their ideas, record those that seem to have promise. Your final design recommendations will be communicated through a memo and sketches to the members of the architectural design committee. In that memo, you must be sure to justify or explain your recommendation. Be sure to give credit in the memo for ideas that came from colleagues. Problem Log F is the blank memo ready for your use.

▶ Recommendation from another committee member:

Positive and negative consequences:

▶ Recommendation from another committee member:

Positive and negative consequences:

▶ Recommendation from another committee member:

Positive and negative consequences:

3. Thinking about Your Thinking (Metacognition)

Before you write your memo, think about what the committee will be looking for in your work. What do you think they expect as to:

▶ **Clarity:** How will you make your work clear and understandable?

▶ **Depth of understanding:** What will you do to show them how well you understand the religious aspects of the problem?

▶ **Appropriateness:** What geometric designs or tessellations will you recommend? Why are these good choices?

Problem Log F—
Memo Describing Your Final Recommendations

To: Architectural design committee

From: _____

Regarding: Recommendations for the lobby decoration designs

Date: _____

Problem Log F—
Memo Describing Your Final Recommendations

Continue on additional paper if necessary.

Problem-Based Learning Unit 5 ——————————

The Dream Machine

Unit Synopsis

Students have each saved $1100 to purchase computer hardware and software for their dream machine. With that amount, they must buy or construct a functioning system that meets their performance needs. The Internet sites presented in the unit take the students to an electronic computer magazine, online buying services for new PCs and MACs, and an online buying service featuring used computer equipment. The sites should help students determine their equipment and software needs, as well as answer technological- and consumer-oriented questions about computer components. The unit ends with each student completing one or more sales receipts from computer sources that document the components they wish to purchase and their ability to stay within the $1100 budget, including tax and shipping.

A Model Definition of the Problem

How can I assemble a computer system with the performance capabilities I want, taking into consideration my $1100 budget, the equipment components I think I need, and the software I want to use initially with the system?

Subject Matter Objectives

Students will be able to:

- Understand that scarcity of resources necessitates choices at both the personal and societal levels.
- Understand that choices usually involve trade-offs—people can give up buying or doing a little of one thing in order to buy or do a little of something else.
- Understand that not all competition is on the basis of price for identical products, and that non-price competition includes style and quality differences, advertising, customer services, and credit policies.
- Identify the major functions for which the computer will be used.
- Identify basic computer hardware (keyboard, monitor, mouse, drives, case, printer, modems, CPU, video card, and other parts).
- Use sound buying principles for purchasing goods and services.
- Identify basic software for their system (operating system, word processing, browser, and others).
- Design a solution or product taking into account needs and constraints.

PBL Unit 5

The Dream Machine?

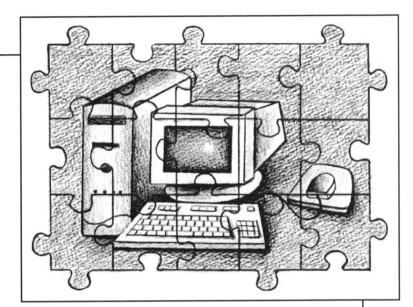

The Situation

You put the bank statement down on your desk. The money you have saved plus the small amount left in your checking account adds up to $1100. This is just what you planned to spend on your dream machine. Eleven hundred dollars for the computer you have been dreaming about.

The timing is perfect. You need the machine because classes will be starting at the community college soon. Even your collection of games has outgrown the old machine.

Almost everything in the old computer was bought secondhand, from friends moving up to new components. Nothing is worth saving.

Your Stake in the Problem

You have $1100 to spend on a new computer, peripherals, and software. Your conscience and your budget will not allow you to spend a penny more, tax and shipping included. What will you buy and where will you buy it?

Problem Log A—
What Is This Problem About?

1. Issues in the Problem

From what you know so far, list three important issues or elements you think are involved in the problem. These questions can help you think about possible issues.

▶ Why is spending $1100 a problem? In what ways will the new computer be used? What components do you need? What might be the consequences if you don't make good decisions about what to buy? What do you need to think about when deciding what to buy?

Issue 1:

Issue 2:

Issue 3:

2. Beginning Your Investigation of the Problem

You need a deeper understanding of the issues in this problem before you can decide on what to buy and from where to buy it. Knowing where to look for information will also be important. List four questions you should answer in order to get a better understanding of the problem.

Question 1:

Question 2:

Question 3:

Question 4:

3. Thinking about Your Thinking (Metacognition)

Your stake in this problem comes from being a consumer faced with a fairly expensive decision. Because you are responsible for this decision and face the consequences of your actions, what skills and attitudes do you need to bring to the investigation?

Expert problem solvers frequently examine their own thinking. One thing they want to keep checking on is their own biases. Why is it important to know what biases you bring to the investigation of a problem? How might bias be involved in the purchase of computer equipment? What are your personal biases as you approach this problem?

Problem Log B— Searching for Relevant, Reliable Information

1. Deepening Your Understanding of the Problem

Clearly state the question you want to answer. If the question seems big and complex, break it into smaller questions. Answering the smaller questions might answer the bigger question.

▶ Your question:

▶ Smaller questions:

2. Searching the Internet

The four Web sites below contain information about your problem. They were found by searching the Internet using the keywords or phrases in bold type. Visit one or more of the sites. Collect relevant, reliable information that helps answer your question.

> **Keywords or phrases: "buying" + "computer"**
>
> **Site 1:** http://www.nextag.com/serv/macbuy/custom/c1/index.html
>
> **Site 2:** http://www.lycos.com/computers
>
> **Site 3:** http://www.zdnet.com/products
>
> **Site 4:** http://www.zdnet.com/pcmag

3. Information from Your First Internet Search

At the top of a sheet of paper, write the three lines found below. Copy the exact URL for the site you are visiting after the line "Internet site." Find the owner of the site, if you can, and add that information after "Owner or controller of the site." Then record relevant information about your question after "Important information." If you visit more than one Internet site, use a separate sheet of paper to record information from each site.

Internet site:

Owner or controller of the site:

Important information:

4. Summarizing What You Learned

After collecting relevant information at a site, summarize what you have learned by answering the question or questions you wrote down at the beginning of your search.

5. Thinking about Your Thinking (Metacognition)

Expert problem solvers make sure the information they use is relevant and reliable. How did you decide if the information you discovered was relevant? How did you decide if it was reliable? What clues at a Web site helped you decide if the information was reliable?

The Internet and Problem-Based Learning, © 2000 Zephyr Press, Tucson, Arizona

Problem Log C—
Thinking about Possible Designs

1. Using Information Found by Others

As you discuss what was found on the Internet, record important ideas and how they might be useful in the spaces below. If you are concerned about the relevance and reliability of information being shared, find out where it came from, when it was created, and if any strong bias could be found at the Web site.

▶ Idea:

How might this be useful?

▶ Idea:

How might this be useful?

▶ Idea:

How might this be useful?

2. Defining the Problem

Before trying to solve a problem, it must be defined. What is the problem you need to resolve?

▶ I need to:

I must take into consideration:

1.

2.

▶ Any other factors?

3. Searching for More Information

New information is likely to produce new questions. In the space below, build a new question based on information you have heard so far. Below the question, enter keywords or phrases that are likely to lead you to information that will help you answer the question.

▶ New question:

▶ Keywords and phrases to guide your search:

4. Thinking about Your Thinking (Metacognition)

Problem solving is challenging work. What have you noticed about yourself during this problem regarding each of these characteristics?

▶ Persistence

▶ Precision

▶ Bias

Problem Log D—
A Second Search of the Internet

1. Digging Deeper into the Problem

Information from your first search of the Internet probably helped answer a number of questions about the issues in this problem. New questions have probably come up too. Using the question you wrote for Problem Log C or a brand new question, dig deeper into this problem using one of the options listed below. Report your new findings on another sheet of paper.

▶ Your question:

▶ *Option A:* Look back at the four Web sites listed in Problem Log B. If you think there might be information at any of these sites that can help you answer your question, go to that site.

▶ *Option B:* Go back to one of the Web sites listed in Problem Log B. Find links to other Web sites listed on the site you are visiting. Check out one or more of the links by placing the mouse arrow on a link and clicking.

▶ *Option C:* Select a search engine and start a new search of the Web by typing in keywords or phrases you listed in Problem Log C.

2. Information from Your Second Internet Search

Record relevant information found during your search on another sheet of paper. Organize the information according to the sites you visited.

Internet site:

Owner or controller of the site:

Important information:

3. Thinking about Your Thinking (Metacognition)

It is likely you still do not thoroughly understand some issues in the problem. But you need to start making some decisions. Problem solvers are often faced with problems that contain unresolved issues or arguments. What issues or questions about computer capabilities, components, or software are still unclear to you? How can you make choices if some issues still need to be resolved?

The Internet and Problem-Based Learning, © 2000 Zephyr Press, Tucson, Arizona

Problem Log E—
Building Solutions

1. More Than One Solution

It is likely that complex, real-world problems can be resolved by more than one action. In fact, a number of actions or solutions will probably be needed to resolve a real problem. Space is provided below for two possible choices involving computer components. Be sure to present both positive and negative consequences that could result from each of your choices. Use additional paper if necessary.

▶ A choice you might make:

Positive consequences:

1.

2.

Negative consequences:

1.

2.

▶ A choice you might make:

Positive consequences:

1.

2.

Negative consequences:

1.

2.

2. Recommendations from Other Members of the Class

As members of your class share their ideas, record those that seem to have promise. The components of your dream machine will be communicated through completed sales receipts from each place where you plan to buy components. With each sales receipt, justify or explain why you chose each component and the site from which you will purchase it. Problem Log F is a blank sales receipt. Make copies of the sheet if you purchase computer components from more than one source.

▶ Recommendation from a classmate:

Positive and negative consequences:

▶ Recommendation from a classmate:

Positive and negative consequences:

▶ Recommendation from a classmate:

Positive and negative consequences:

3. Thinking about Your Thinking (Metacognition)

Before you fill out sales receipts, think again about what will make a dream machine for you by answering the following questions. Use additional paper if necessary.

▶ What are the most important things you want your dream machine to do?

▶ How well did you research the issues?

▶ How satisfied are you with your dream machine? Did you have to make compromises in constructing your computer?

Problem Log F—
Sales Receipt for Computer Equipment or Software

Customer Name: _____ Date: _____

Purchased From: _____

Quantity	Item	Unit Price	Amount
		Subtotal	
		Tax	
		Shipping	
		Total Amount Due	

Problem Log F—
Inventory of Items Purchased

Item	Total Amount Paid
Total Amount for New System ▶	

Remember the total amount for your new system cannot exceed $1100.

Problem-Based Learning Unit 6 ———————————

Sink It to the Bottom

Unit Synopsis

Students take on the role of scientists, selected by a major petroleum company and environmental activists presently occupying the oil platform, Brent Spar. The platform is to be decommissioned, and the company wants to scuttle it to the bottom of the North Sea. Company representatives claim it is the cheapest and safest way to get rid of the obsolete floating container, adding that it will provide habitat for fish. The environmental group claims scuttling the tank will create a large-scale environmental disaster. Members of the group have occupied the tank and refuse to leave until an environmentally safe method of decommissioning is found. The activists have also organized a boycott of the oil company's products in Europe. In a week, the students, as scientists, must present their evaluation of the company's plan and make recommendations regarding the safe decommissioning of the platform.

A Model Definition of the Problem

How can the Brent Spar be decommissioned in a way that is cost effective for the company, avoids excessive negative impact on the environment, and can act as a model for future decommissioning?

Subject Matter Objectives

Students will be able to:

- Understand that all organisms, including the human species, are part of and depend on two main global food chains—one starts with microscopic ocean plants and the other begins with land plants.
- Understand that all of the populations living together (known as a community) plus the physical factors with which they interact, compose a local ecosystem.
- Understand that humans are increasingly modifying ecosystems, possibly threatening global stability and causing potentially irreversible damage to those systems.
- Understand that when an element has atoms that differ in the number of neutrons, these atoms are called different isotopes of the element.
- Understand that results of scientific inquiry—new knowledge and methods— emerge from investigations and public communication among scientists; the nature of scientific review is guided by logical and empirical criteria, and by connections between natural phenomena, investigations, and the historical body of scientific knowledge.
- Understand that technological solutions have trade-offs, such as safety, cost, efficiency, and appearance; risk is part of living in a highly technological world.
- Understand that technological solutions have intended benefits and unintended consequences; some consequences can be predicted, but others cannot.

Name _____ Date _____ Class Period _____

PBL Unit 6
Sink It to the Bottom

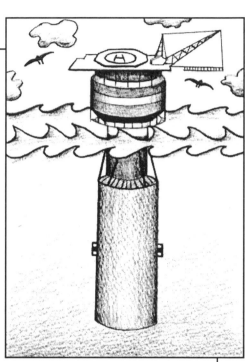

The Situation

Named Brent Spar by its owner, the Shell Oil Company, the 40-story oil storage tank is easy to spot—even in the dark choppy water of the North Sea. Its giant carcass, towering more than 90 feet above the surface of the water, is anchored at 60 degrees north latitude, 50 kilometers west of the Shetland Islands. It has been there since June 1995. According to Shell Oil plans, the storage tank should have been disposed of by now. But environmental activists have gotten involved and the obsolete tank has no place to go.

The Brent Spar is now your problem. The parties in the controversy have agreed that they need impartial experts' recommendations for decommissioning the tank. They want these experts to determine the impact on the ocean's environment of scuttling the platform and sinking it to the bottom of the sea, somewhere close to where it is now anchored. This is the option favored by the oil company. The activists fear the material left over in the tank and its pipes will cause a monumental environmental disaster if it is released into the ocean.

Your Stake in the Problem

You are one of the scientists asked to make recommendations on what to do with the Brent Spar. Your recommendations, and those of your fellow scientists, are due in a week.

Problem Log A—
What Is This Problem About?

1. Issues in the Problem

From what you know so far, list three important issues or elements you think are involved in the problem. These questions can help you think about possible issues.

▶ How did this controversy get started? What do environmental activists fear about the Brent Spar? What's the science in the problem? What might be the consequences for the environment if the activists are right? What are the consequences if they are wrong?

Issue 1:

Issue 2:

Issue 3:

2. Beginning Your Investigation

You need a deeper understanding of the issues in the problem before you can recommend solutions. List four questions you should answer in order to get a better understanding of the problem.

Question 1:

Question 2:

Question 3:

Question 4:

3. Thinking about Your Thinking (Metacognition)

Your stake in this problem comes from being a member of a scientific team. Based on your authority and responsibility as a scientist, what skills and attitudes will you need to bring to the investigation of this problem?

Expert problem solvers frequently examine their own thinking. One thing they want to keep checking on is their own bias. Why is it important to know what biases you bring to the investigation of a problem? What are your personal biases as you approach this problem?

Problem Log B—
Searching for Relevant, Reliable Information

1. Deepening Your Understanding of the Problem

Clearly state the question you want to answer. If the question seems big and complex, break it into smaller questions. Answering the smaller questions might answer the bigger question.

▶ Your question:

▶ Smaller questions:

2. Searching the Internet

The four Web sites below contain information about your problem. They were found by searching the Internet using the keywords or phrases in bold type. Visit one or more of the sites. Collect relevant, reliable information that helps answer your questions.

Keywords or phrases: "Brent Spar" + "toxic chemicals"

Site 1: http://news2.thdo.bbc.co.uk/low/english/world/newsid_51000/51360.stm

Site 2: http://www.shell.com/home

Site 3: http://greenpeace.org/~comms/brent/brent.html

Site 4: http://www.scorecard.org/chemical-profiles

3. Information from Your First Internet Search

At the top of a sheet of paper, write the three lines found below. Copy the exact URL for the site you are visiting after the line "Internet site." Find the owner of the site, if you can, and add that information after "Owner or controller of the site." Then record relevant information about your question after "Important information." If you visit more than one Internet site, use a separate sheet of paper to record information from each site.

Internet site:

Owner or controller of the site:

Important information:

4. Summarizing What You Learned

After collecting relevant information at a site, summarize what you have learned by answering the question or questions you wrote down at the beginning of your search.

5. Thinking about Your Thinking (Metacognition)

Expert problem solvers make sure the information they use is relevant and reliable. How did you decide if the information you discovered was relevant? How did you decide if it was reliable? What clues at a Web site helped you decide if the information was reliable?

Problem Log C—
Thinking about the Brent Spar

1. Using Information Found by Others

As you discuss what was found on the Internet, record important ideas and how they might be used in the spaces below. If you are concerned about the relevance or reliability of information being shared, find out where it came from, when it was created, and if any strong bias could be found at the Web site.

▶ Idea:

How might this be useful?

▶ Idea:

How might this be useful?

▶ Idea:

How might this be useful?

2. Defining the Problem

Before trying to solve a problem, it must be defined. What is the problem you and the other scientists need to resolve?

▶ We need to:

We must take into consideration:

1.

2.

▶ Any other factors?

3. Searching for More Information

New information is likely to produce new questions. In the space below, build a new question based on information you have heard so far. Below the question, enter keywords or phrases that are likely to lead you to information that will help you answer the question.

▶ New question:

▶ Keywords and phrases to guide your search:

4. Thinking about Your Thinking (Metacognition)

Problem solving is challenging work. What have you noticed about yourself during this problem regarding each of these characteristics?

▶ Persistence

▶ Precision

▶ Open-mindedness

Problem Log D—
A Second Search of the Internet

1. Digging Deeper into the Problem

Information from your first search of the Internet probably helped answer a number of questions about the issues in this problem. New questions have probably come up too. Using the question you wrote for Problem Log C or a brand new question, dig deeper into this problem using one of the options listed below. Report your new findings on another sheet of paper.

▶ Your question:

▶ *Option A:* Look back at the Web sites listed in Problem Log B. If you think there might be information at any of these sites that can help you answer your question, go to that site.

▶ *Option B:* Go back to one of the Web sites listed in Problem Log B. Find links to other Web sites listed on the site you are visiting. Check out one or more of the links by placing the mouse arrow on a link and clicking.

▶ *Option C:* Select a search engine and start a new search of the Web by typing in keywords or phrases you listed in Problem Log C.

2. Information from Your Second Internet Search

Record relevant information found during your search on another sheet of paper. Organize the information according to the sites you visited.

Internet site:

Owner or controller of the site:

Important information:

3. Thinking about Your Thinking (Metacognition)

It is likely you still do not understand some issues in the problem. But the parties sponsoring the investigation want your recommendations soon. Experts are often asked to solve problems that contain unresolved issues or arguments. What issues or questions about the storage tank are still unclear to you? How can you make recommendations if some issues still need to be resolved?

Problem Log E—
Building Solutions

1. More Than One Solution

Since it is possible for complex, real-world problems to have more than one solution, space is provided on this page for two possible recommendations. List your recommendations and the positive and negative consequences that are likely to result from each. Use additional paper if necessary.

▶ First recommendation:

   Positive consequences:

   1.

   2.

   Negative consequences:

   1.

   2.

▶ Second recommendation:

   Positive consequences:

   1.

   2.

   Negative consequences:

   1.

   2.

2. Recommendations from Other Members of the Team

As others share their ideas, record those that seem likely to contribute to a recommendation on what to do with the Brent Spar. Your final recommendations will be collected in a memo addressed to the stakeholders in this controversy. In that memo, you must be sure to justify or explain why each recommendation is a good or right thing to do. Be sure to give credit in the memo for ideas that came from other scientists. Problem Log F is the blank memo ready for your use.

▶ Recommendation from another scientist:

Positive and negative consequences:

▶ Recommendation from another scientist:

Positive and negative consequences:

▶ Recommendation from another scientist:

Positive and negative consequences:

3. Thinking about Your Thinking (Metacognition)

Before you write your memo, think about what the parties in the controversy will be looking for in your work. What do you think they expect as to:

▶ **Clarity:** How will you make your work clear and understandable?

▶ **Depth of understanding:** What will you do to show them how well you understand the problem? What costs are associated with further delay in making a decision?

▶ **Fairness:** How will you make sure the parties in the controversy have confidence in your recommendations?

Problem Log F—
Memo Describing Final Recommendations

To: Stakeholders in the Brent Spar controversy

From: _____

Regarding: Recommendations for decommissioning the Brent Spar

Date: _____

Problem Log F—
Memo Describing Final Recommendations

Continue on additional paper if necessary.

Problem-Based Learning Unit 7 _____

What Should Be Done about Galileo?

Unit Synopsis

As officials of the Inquisition in 1633, the students must decide what to do with Galileo Galilei. Galileo's writing supports the theories of Copernicus. Both men argue that the planets revolve around the sun, making it the center of our solar system. This belief contradicts the teaching of the Catholic Church at that time. As officials of the Inquisition, students are charged with upholding the teachings of the church and dealing with heretics who challenge those ideas. They must consider the ideas of Galileo and compare them with those of the church in 1633. When they recognize the difference between the two sets of ideas, they must decide what to do about it. The fact that the Holy Roman Catholic Church is also in a gigantic struggle with the newly emerging Protestant movement for the faith of people all across Europe complicates the situation.

A Model Definition of the Problem

As an official of the Inquisition, what should I recommend that high Church officials do about the scholar Galileo and his potentially heretical writing? My recommendation must consider: 1) Galileo's ideas in relation to accepted Church teaching; 2) the role of the Protestant movement in Church attitudes toward heresy; 3) Galileo's social status.

Subject Matter Objectives

Students will be able to:

- Understand the patterns of religious affiliation in Europe in the early 17th century, and factors that led some populations to embrace the Protestant Reformation while others rejected it.
- Understand the coexistence of the new scientific rationalism in 17th- and 18th-century Europe with traditional learning and rituals (e.g., factors that prevented widespread acceptance of scientific method; the arguments and evidence used in the trial of Galileo to prove him "innocent" or "guilty;" the major features of the scientific revolution in major fields of endeavor).

Name _____ Date _____ Class Period _____

PBL Unit 7

What Should Be Done about Galileo?

The Situation

The year is 1633. It is a time of great turmoil for the Catholic Church. The Protestant Reformation has changed the religious and political face of Europe. The Church of Rome is struggling to maintain its traditions and keep its members obedient to its laws. Heresy is everywhere.

The Inquisition, an arm of the church established to find and punish heretics, has been extremely active during this time of upheaval. Now it has a new case to consider: possible heresy committed by Galileo Galilei.

Galileo has just published the book, *Dialogue on the Two Great World Systems*. In it, he supports the view of Copernicus that the planets, including the earth, revolve around the sun. However, according to the church, the sun and planets revolve around the earth. Because Copernicus' book states that the earth is not the center of the universe, it has been on the Index of Forbidden Books since 1616. Now Galileo seems to be urging the people to accept the view of Copernicus.

Your Stake in the Problem

You are an official of the Inquisition. It is your job to decide what to do with Galileo. If you believe his writing and actions fit under the definition of heresy, you could bring him to trial. If he is found guilty, he could be put to death. But there might be a complication. Galileo is a friend of some high church officials. What will you do with this scholar, Galileo?

Problem Log A—
What Is This Problem About?

1. Issues in the Problem

From what you know so far, list three important issues or elements you think are involved in the problem. These questions can help you think about possible issues.

▶ How did this controversy get started? Why is the Catholic Church concerned about Copernicus, Galileo, and their ideas? What authority and responsibility do you have in this situation? What might be the consequences for taking action against Galileo? What might the consequences be if no action is taken? What is the Inquisition?

Issue 1:

Issue 2:

Issue 3:

2. Beginning Your Investigation

You need a deeper understanding of the issues in the problem before you can make a recommendation regarding Galileo. List four questions you and fellow members of the Inquisition should answer in order to get a better understanding of the problem.

Question 1:

Question 2:

Question 3:

Question 4:

3. Thinking about Your Thinking (Metacognition)

Your stake in this problem comes from being a member of the Inquisition. Because of your authority and responsibility, what skills and attitudes will you need to bring to the investigation of this problem?

Expert problem solvers frequently examine their own thinking. One thing they want to keep checking on is their own bias. Why is it important to know what biases you bring to the investigation of a problem? What are your personal biases as you approach this problem?

Problem Log B—
Searching for Relevant, Reliable Information

1. Deepening Your Understanding of the Problem

Clearly state the question you want to answer. If the question seems big and complex, break it into smaller questions. Answering the smaller questions might answer the bigger question.

▶ Your question:

▶ Smaller questions:

2. Searching the Internet

The four Web sites below contain information about your problem. They were found by searching the Internet using the keywords or phrases in bold type. Visit one or more of the sites. Collect relevant, reliable information that helps answer your questions.

> **Keywords or phrases: "Galileo" + "inquisition"**
>
> **Site 1:** http://newadvent.org/cathen
>
> **Site 2:** http://es.rice.edu/ES/humsoc/Galileo/galileo_timeline.html
>
> **Site 3:** http://www.fordham.edu/halsall/mod/1630galileo.html
>
> **Site 4:** http://catholiceducation.org

3. Information from Your First Internet Search

At the top of a sheet of paper, write the three lines found below. Copy the exact URL for the site you are visiting after the line "Internet site." Find the owner of the site, if you can, and add that information after "Owner or controller of the site." Then record relevant information about your question after "Important information." If you visit more than one Internet site, use a separate sheet of paper to record information from each site.

Internet site:

Owner or controller of the site:

Important information:

4. Summarizing What You Learned

After collecting relevant information at a site, summarize what you have learned by answering the question or questions you wrote down at the beginning of your search.

5. Thinking about Your Thinking (Metacognition)

Expert problem solvers make sure the information they use is relevant and reliable. How did you decide if the information you discovered was relevant? How did you decide if it was reliable? What clues at a Web site helped you decide if the information was reliable?

The Internet and Problem-Based Learning, © 2000 Zephyr Press, Tucson, Arizona

Problem Log C— ## Thinking about Galileo and the Inquisition

1. Using Information Found by Others

As you discuss what was found on the Internet, record important ideas and how they might be used in the spaces below. If you are concerned about the relevance or reliability of information being shared, find out where it came from, when it was created, and if any strong bias could be found at the Web site.

▶ Idea:

How might this be useful?

▶ Idea:

How might this be useful?

▶ Idea:

How might this be useful?

2. Defining the Problem

Before trying to solve a problem, it must be defined. What is the problem you and the other officials need to resolve?

▶ I need to:

I must take into consideration:

1.

2.

▶ Any other factors?

3. Searching for More Information

New information is likely to produce new questions. In the space below, build a new question based on information you have heard so far. Below the question, enter keywords or phrases that are likely to lead you to information that will help you answer the question.

▶ New question:

▶ Keywords and phrases to guide your search:

4. Thinking about Your Thinking (Metacognition)

Problem solving is challenging work. What have you noticed about yourself during this problem regarding each of these characteristics?

▶ Persistence

▶ Precision

Problem Log D—
A Second Search of the Internet

1. Digging Deeper into the Problem

Information from your first search of the Internet probably helped answer a number of questions about the issues in this problem. New questions have probably come up too. Using the question you wrote for Problem Log C or a brand new question, dig deeper into this problem using one of the options listed below. Report your new findings on another sheet of paper.

▶   Your question:

▶   *Option A:* Look back at the Web sites listed in Problem Log B. If you think there might be information at any of these sites that can help you answer your question, go to that site.

▶   *Option B:* Go back to one of the Web sites listed in Problem Log B. Find links to other Web sites listed on the site you are visiting. Check out one or more of the links by placing the mouse arrow on a link and clicking.

▶   *Option C:* Select a search engine and start a new search of the Web by typing in keywords or phrases you listed in Problem Log C.

2. Information from Your Second Internet Search

Record relevant information found during your search on another sheet of paper. Organize the information according to the sites you visited.

Internet site:

Owner or controller of the site:

Important information:

3. Thinking about Your Thinking (Metacognition)

It is likely you still do not understand some issues in the problem. But your superiors are going to want your recommendation soon. Experts are often asked to solve problems that have unresolved issues or arguments in them. What issues or questions are still unclear to you? How can you make a recommendation if some issues still need to be resolved?

The Internet and Problem-Based Learning, © 2000 Zephyr Press, Tucson, Arizona

Problem Log E—
Building Solutions

1. More Than One Solution

Since it is possible for complex, real-world problems to have more than one solution, space is provided for a number of possible recommendations. In the spaces below, briefly describe two recommendations you believe can help resolve the problem involving Galileo. For each recommendation, list the positive and negative consequences they are likely to produce. Use additional paper if necessary.

▶ First recommendation:

Positive consequences:

1.

2.

Negative consequences:

1.

2.

▶ Second recommendation:

Positive consequences:

1.

2.

Negative consequences:

1.

2.

2. Recommendations from Other Members of the Inquisition

As members share their ideas for recommendations, record those that seem like good ideas. Your final recommendations regarding Galileo will be made in a letter to Church officials leading the Inquisition. In that letter, you must be sure to justify or explain why each recommendation is the right thing to do. If you decide to indict Galileo, be sure you describe why he is a heretic. Problem Log F is a blank letter form ready for your use.

▶ Recommendation from another member of the Inquisition:

Positive and negative consequences:

▶ Recommendation from another member of the Inquisition:

Positive and negative consequences:

▶ Recommendation from another member of the Inquisition:

Positive and negative consequences:

The Internet and Problem-Based Learning, © 2000 Zephyr Press, Tucson, Arizona

3. Thinking about Your Thinking (Metacognition)

Before you write your letter, think about what the church leaders will be looking for in your work. What do they expect as to:

▶ **Clarity:** How will you make your ideas clear?

▶ **Depth of understanding:** How will you show them how well you understand the problem?

▶ **Loyalty to the Church:** How will your recommendation help control heretical thinking?

Problem Log F—
Letter Presenting a Recommendation Regarding Galileo

To the shepherds leading our flock through terrible times; honorable and pious men, take notice of this recommendation in the matter of Galileo Galilei.

Problem Log F—
Letter Presenting a Recommendation Regarding Galileo

Continue on additional paper if necessary.

Problem-Based Learning Unit 8

Legends of Rock and Roll

Unit Synopsis

As writers for a popular entertainment magazine students must create a 250-word article for this month's issue that introduces the magazine's new Legends of Rock & Roll gallery and its first inductees, the Rolling Stones. Specifically, the articles must explain why the Rolling Stones were selected as the first inductees, and what three criteria were used for the selection. The criteria are important because the magazine plans to induct future legends based upon periodic polls of the readership. The criteria will be stressed with the readers before each polling period begins. The students are responsible for researching their subject and developing the content of the article (history and significance of the Rolling Stones, criteria for future selections, background on the gallery itself) so readers can understand it. They must write an interesting article that fits the allotted space in the magazine.

A Model Definition of the Problem

What should I say in my article announcing the induction of the Rolling Stones as the first Legend of Rock & Roll that clearly explains the reasons the Stones were selected as the first inductees, lays out the criteria readers should use in making future selections, and is interesting reading for the people who pick up our magazine?

Subject Matter Objectives

Students will be able to:

- Demonstrate competence in writing expository essays (i.e., synthesize information from a variety of sources, select appropriate techniques to develop the main idea, cite an anecdote to provide an example, and provide interesting facts about a subject).
- Write compositions that are clearly focused for specific audiences.
- Demonstrate competence in writing persuasive essays (i.e., clearly articulate a position through a thesis sentence, back up assertions with criteria, and develop arguments using a variety of methods).
- Demonstrate competence in the stylistic and rhetorical aspects of writing (i.e., transitional devices, sentence structure, descriptive language, supportive details, and imaginative vocabulary).
- Write essays that have no significant errors according to the grammatical and mechanical conventions of compositions.

PBL Unit 8

Legends of Rock & Roll

The Situation

A week left and still no story! The music editor for one of the most popular entertainment magazines in the business has already given two writers the assignment, but neither has produced what she wants. Six months ago, the magazine decided to build a gallery dedicated to the legends of rock and roll. It will be located in the lobby of the magazine's New York headquarters. Every year, the magazine's readers will select five individuals or groups to be inducted into the gallery. The magazine wants people selected according to criteria that identify them as pioneers or super stars. The first selection to the gallery will be done by the magazine and announced in a special article in next month's issue.

Time is running out. If a 250-word story introducing the first selection to the gallery, the Rolling Stones, is not ready in a week, the opening of the gallery will need to be rescheduled. This would not be good for the magazine. The editor in charge of producing the story would probably lose his or her job.

Your Stake in the Problem

The editor has given you the job of writing the story that introduces the Rolling Stones as the first members of the legend's gallery. The story must explain why the Rolling Stones were chosen first for the gallery, and present three criteria that the readers should use in selecting future members. The editor wants your story in a week.

Problem Log A—
What Is This Problem About?

1. Issues in the Problem

From what you know so far, list three important issues or elements you think are involved in the problem. These questions can help you think about possible issues.

▶ What does the magazine expect? Why have they chosen you? Why might the Rolling Stones be considered true legends? What criteria identify a legend? Who reads the magazine? What is rock and roll anyway?

Issue 1:

Issue 2:

Issue 3:

2. Beginning Your Investigation

You need a deeper understanding of the issues in the problem before you can begin writing a solution—the 250-word article. List four questions you should answer in order to get a better understanding of the problem.

Question 1:

Question 2:

Question 3:

Question 4:

3. Thinking about Your Thinking (Metacognition)

Your stake in this problem comes from being a writer who understands rock and roll and produces under time pressure. Because of your authority and responsibility, what skills and attitudes will you need to bring to the resolution of this problem?

Expert problem solvers frequently examine their own thinking. One thing they want to keep checking on is their own bias. Why is it important to know what biases you bring to the resolution of a problem? What are your personal biases as you approach this problem?

Problem Log B—
Searching for Relevant, Reliable Information

1. Deepening Your Understanding of the Problem

Clearly state the question you want to answer. If the question seems big and complex, break it into smaller questions. Answering the smaller questions might answer the bigger question.

▶ Your question:

▶ Smaller questions:

2. Searching the Internet

The four Web sites below contain information about your problem. They were found by searching the Internet using the keywords or phrases in bold type. Visit one or more of the sites. Collect relevant, reliable information that helps answer your questions.

Keywords or phrases: "Rolling Stones"

Site 1: http://rockhall.com/hof/inductee.asp?id=182

Site 2: http://www.allmusic.com/index.html

Site 3: http://music.lycos.com

Site 4: http://www.rollingstone.com

3. Information from Your First Internet Search

At the top of a sheet of paper, write the three lines found below. Copy the exact URL for the site you are visiting after the line "Internet site." Find the owner of the site, if you can, and add that information after "Owner or controller of the site." Then record relevant information about your question after "Important information." If you visit more than one Internet site, use a separate sheet of paper to record information from each site.

Internet site:

Owner or controller of the site:

Important information:

4. Summarizing What You Learned

After collecting relevant information at a site, summarize what you have learned by answering the question or questions you wrote down at the beginning of your search.

5. Thinking about Your Thinking (Metacognition)

Expert problem solvers make sure the information they use is relevant and reliable. How did you decide if the information you discovered was relevant? How did you decide if it was reliable? What clues at a Web site helped you decide if the information was reliable?

Problem Log C—
Thinking about Writing the Article

1. Using Information Found by Others

As you discuss what was found on the Internet, record important ideas and how they might be used in the spaces below. If you are concerned about the relevance or reliability of information being shared, find out where it came from, when it was created, and if any strong bias could be found at the Web site.

▶ Idea:

How might this be useful?

▶ Idea:

How might this be useful?

▶ Idea:

How might this be useful?

2. Defining the Problem

Before trying to solve a problem, it must be defined. What is the problem you need to resolve?

▶ I need to:

I must take into consideration:

1.

2.

▶ Any other factors?

3. Searching for More Information

New information is likely to produce new questions. In the space below, build a new question based on information you have heard so far. Below the question, enter keywords or phrases that are likely to lead you to information that will help you answer the question.

▶ New question:

▶ Keywords and phrases to guide your search:

4. Thinking about Your Thinking (Metacognition)

Did you ever think of journalists and writers as problem solvers before? What have you noticed about yourself during this problem regarding each of these traits?

▶ Persistence

▶ Precision

▶ Creativity

Problem Log D—
A Second Search of the Internet

1. Digging Deeper into the Problem

Information from your first search of the Internet probably helped answer a number of questions about the issues in this problem. New questions have probably come up too. Using the question you wrote for Problem Log C or a brand new question, dig deeper into this problem using one of the options listed below. Report your new findings on another sheet of paper.

▶ Your question:

▶ *Option A:* Look back at the Web sites listed in Problem Log B. If you think there might be information at any of these sites that can help you answer your question, go to that site.

▶ *Option B:* Go back to one of the Web sites listed in Problem Log B. Find links to other Web sites listed on the site you are visiting. Check out one or more of the links by placing the mouse arrow on a link and clicking.

▶ *Option C:* Select a search engine and start a new search of the Web by typing in keywords or phrases you listed in Problem Log C.

2. Information from Your Second Internet Search

Record relevant information found during your search on another sheet of paper. Organize the information according to the sites you visited.

Internet site:

Owner or controller of the site:

Important information:

3. Thinking about Your Thinking (Metacognition)

It is likely you still do not understand some issues in the problem. But the editor wants your story soon. Experts are often asked to solve problems that contain unresolved issues or arguments. What issues or questions about the lives and music of the Rolling Stones are still unclear to you? How can you build a solution, an interesting and informative article, if some issues still need to be resolved?

The Internet and Problem-Based Learning, © 2000 Zephyr Press, Tucson, Arizona

Problem Log E—
Building Solutions

1. More Than One Solution

Since it is possible for complex, real-world problems to have more than one solution, space is provided on this page for two reasons why the Rolling Stones were chosen as the first performers inducted into the new and prestigious gallery. Space can also be used to recommend ideas on how the article itself should be organized. Use additional paper if necessary.

▶ Criteria for selection or idea for the article:

Strengths of the criteria or idea:

1.

2.

Weaknesses of the criteria or idea:

1.

2.

▶ Criteria for selection or idea for the article:

Strengths of the criteria or idea:

1.

2.

Weaknesses of the criteria or idea:

1.

2.

2. Criteria and Ideas from Other Journalists in Class

As members of your class share their ideas, record those that seem useable. Think about strengths and weaknesses of each. You can write your first draft of the article in Problem Log F.

▶ Criteria or idea suggested by another writer:

Its strengths and weaknesses:

▶ Criteria or idea suggested by another writer:

Its strengths and weaknesses:

▶ Criteria or idea suggested by another writer:

Its strengths and weaknesses:

3. Thinking about Your Thinking (Metacognition)

Before you write your article, think about what the editor will be looking for in your work. What do you think she expects as to:

▶ **Clarity and creativity:** How clearly and creatively will you present your ideas?

▶ **Depth of understanding:** How deeply do you understand the events and music that make up the lives and careers of the Rolling Stones?

Problem Log F—
Lobby of Legends (Article's Title)

The Internet and Problem-Based Learning, © 2000 Zephyr Press, Tucson, Arizona

Part III
Appendices

Appendix I ———————————————

What Is the Internet?

Introduction

The Internet is many things to many people. To scientists and scholars, the Internet is a way to share resources and publish their research findings quickly. For businesses, it is a way to serve their customers without the customers ever leaving their homes or offices.

For individuals, the Internet serves many other purposes. For shoppers, it is a way to search the country for bargains. For those who seek knowledge, it is a way to find it. For those who wish to visit with others, it is a new way to reach out. For the teacher, it is all of these things and more. Most importantly, the Internet is a means of providing students with information on a scale never before possible.

In order to use the Internet productively, it is necessary to know something about what it is and how it works.

Defining the Internet

The Internet is a worldwide collection of connected computers. The World Wide Web, or Web for short, is a part of the Internet.

The Internet is made up of thousands of individual computers that are all connected by means of telephone lines, cables, and satellite transmissions. All of the machines are connected in order to communicate with one another. The connected computers form networks. Networks can be small or gigantic, based on the number of connected machines.

Although governments, businesses, and other groups or agencies support the Internet financially, they do not manage it. The Internet is a remarkable example of individual responsibility. It is managed by the people who use it. Many of the people who manage the network are volunteers who cooperate to make it work. They form a community the likes of which has never been seen before.

Those who use the Internet are expected to behave civilly, respect the property and privacy of others, and contribute to the Internet community when they can.

The fact that the Internet is based on cooperative behavior and managed by the people who use it means that it is changing all the time.

It also means that no one pays for the whole thing—everyone pays for his or her part. The smaller networks—for example, those in schools—decide how to connect their computers together and pay for these interconnections. An Internet Service Provider (ISP) that connects the computers in the schools to the Internet most often provides this service.

Just as you do not have to know how a motor works in order to drive a car, you do not have to know how the collection of networks that make up the Internet works to use it. What you do have to know is what to do if something seems to be working poorly.

If you are an individual Internet user and something goes wrong, you get in touch with the ISP that provides the connection between your home computer and the Internet. Schools that are networked usually have their own technology support person, sometimes even a network operations center (NOC). If you do not know whom to contact when something goes wrong in your school, you should find out before you begin the projects in this book.

What Type of Equipment Do You Need to Use the Internet?

In order to work on the Internet you must have a computer, modem, and a service provider.

Most computers are connected to the Internet by means of an ISP, a commercial organization that sells access to the Internet. Service providers play an important role in the Internet. Examples of large ISPs include America Online, Compuserv, and many telephone companies.

When you sign up with an ISP you have access to the Internet plus many other services provided by the company. The role of the service provider is to set up gateways that allow you, the subscriber, easy and trouble-free access to the Internet.

The equipment needs for working with the Internet are relatively simple. For most users, a computer with a good high-speed modem will do. After that it is a matter of deciding which services you want from the long list of available providers. When it comes to classroom use of the Internet, all of these decisions have probably been made for you. Your job will be to fit the tools found on the Internet to your students and your curricular responsibilities.

Software Makes the Internet Work

There are many things you can do on the Internet. You can transfer files; you can communicate with email or in chat groups. You can use another computer as though it were your own. You can find information of all kinds. Doing each of these things could require a different set of software programs that follow very specific rules.

Suppose that you are shopping for a new printer to add to your computer system. You might want to learn about the features and prices of printers by visiting the electronic versions of computer magazines located on the Web. One of the magazines contains a special section evaluating printers like the one you are considering. Instead of reading the lengthy article while connected to the Internet, you decide to download it to your machine. Once this has been accomplished, you can disconnect from the Internet, print the file containing the printer article, and read about your printer choices with your feet up on the couch. What you would be doing is shifting a copy of the file that contains the printer article from the remote computer to your own machine. This is an example of transferring a file.

To do this transfer, you are using the file transfer protocol (FTP). It is the set of rules that are used to move files from one computer to the other. Think of the FTP as a service that lets you connect to another computer on the Internet, browse through the files that are available on that computer, then either send or get files to or from it.

The Internet allows for other kinds of communications too, including electronic mail (email), discussion (chat) groups, or playing games (such as chess or bridge) with others.

Electronic mail (email) is a message in the form of a file sent from your account (machine) to someone else's account (machine) on the Internet. The file must be in a certain form and follow certain rules. Fortunately, most of these rules are transparent to the user. Many available software programs allow for easy sending and receipt of electronic mail.

Discussion or chat groups are another Internet resource. Many teachers use them to exchange ideas, lesson plans, textbook reviews, and almost everything that interests a good teacher.

To make messages available to a number of people at the same time, mailing lists are used. Without mailing lists, every person in the group would have to send a message to every other person in the group, and keeping track of all this would be cumbersome. Mailing lists make it easy. Special software programs allow you to automatically send your message to everybody on the list.

Discussion groups exist for every conceivable interest. Because they are easy to start, there is no lack of them. Some discussion groups are moderated. This means that somebody looks at every message before it is sent out to members. Other groups are not moderated. This means that no one looks at the messages before they are sent to everyone on the list. Discussion groups without moderators can be a risky resource for student use. There is no way to predict who or what students will meet through this type of discussion group.

News about a particular topic can be communicated to many other people without the use of specific lists. Some of the machines on the Internet are organized into users' networks with the help of Usenet. The software on Usenet sends individual messages, sometimes called articles or postings, from a local computer to all the computers that participate in it. Anybody who subscribes to the group can read and reply to the articles that are submitted.

Telnet software makes it possible for a user to enter other computers that are set up for it. For example, using Telnet, you may simply log onto the computer that has the library card catalog, and use the entire catalog as though it was on your own machine.

There is so much information on the Internet that finding it is often not easy. The software used to find information is called a browser or a search engine. Search engines allow the user to type in a word or phrase. Then the software goes through many of the resources on the Internet and reports back to the user where the material may be found.

The World Wide Web

The World Wide Web is a very special part of the Internet. The Web adds new capabilities to sites. This means that client computers can use pictures, video, sound, and computer animation stored on host computers.

The World Wide Web also has the unique ability to link files and documents on one of its computers to other files and documents on other machines. It has the ability to connect all the other information-retrieval systems together.

The basic technology behind the World Wide Web is hypertext. Hypertext is a way to present information so that when a word or icon on the screen is selected, the computer automatically links to more information about it. This other information could be music, animation, text, programs, or other Web sites.

Hypertext is an extremely powerful information system because there are no limitations on the links. They can point anywhere that the person who set up the Web page wishes. This capability means that virtually each site you visit on the Web opens the door to other sites related to the first.

But the most important way for most people to use the World Wide Web is by means of search engines (browsers). There are many of them, most of them provided free of charge. The power and affordability of browsers is one of the reasons for the incredibly rapid expansion of the World Wide Web.

The World Wide Web has created new opportunities for communicating, working, and learning. Because of what it can do, it has led to the formation of new communities through networks. It has allowed the development of relationships between people scattered throughout the world. For example, human rights activists in Mexico, Zaire, and China can now communicate quickly and cheaply with one another.

The Web's rapid growth, however, has led to a continuing problem for the whole Internet —too much information. For example, the Web browser Yahoo *(www.yahoo.com)* has almost a half a million Web sites stored in a hierarchical directory that you can browse by subject matter. A team of librarians constructed this directory. Yahoo stands for "Yet another hierarchical officious oracle," proving librarians have a sense of humor. Another browser, InfoSeekUltra *(http://www.infoseek.go.com)*, has a directory of about three-quarters of a million Web sites.

None of these search engines has solved the problem of easily finding precisely what you want among the millions of sites on the Web. It is not unusual to type a single word into one of the search engines and get back a list of a million or more sites. Many of these are duplicates, no longer operational, or contain material that is irrelevant.

Navigation has become the biggest problem for the whole Internet. Except for simple tasks, using the Web productively is more than many people can handle. Learning skills to successfully navigate the Internet, then using the information for productive problem solving are important skills for students to master.

Putting It All Together

In order to work on the Internet you or your school needs an account with an ISP. An account means that arrangements have been made to use certain selective services on the Internet.

When you log in you are telling the computer that you want to work on it. It needs to identify you, and that is the reason for your login name. After you log in, you will be asked to type in your password. Most often the people who run the system assign the passwords. Sometimes the host gives them to you, and sometimes you can choose them.

Passwords have many uses on the Internet. Their central purpose is to provide security. That means only letting in people who have the right to use a service or access a file. Schools may use passwords to make sure that only the right person uses certain resources. You will have to check with the policy and procedures in your school or district to find out how security regarding access to the Internet is handled.

The Internet is much more user-friendly today than it was just a few years ago. The resources available over the Internet, especially through the World Wide Web, continue to grow at an astonishing rate, with no signs of slowing down. Teachers approaching the Internet today will find resources that can change forever the way they instruct and continue as learners themselves.

Appendix II _____

How Search Engines Work

There are almost as many definitions of a search engine as there are authors who write about them. For example, search engines are sometimes referred to as browsers, indexes, catalogs, or spiders.

This is because all search engines have three major parts. One part is the spider, or crawler. This is software that crawls or searches the Web compiling data on what it finds. The crawler, or spider, visits Web pages. It scans the pages and follows links to other pages within the same site. Then people search through what the crawlers have found and assign the data to keywords, phrases, or other categories. When we search the Internet using our own keywords, the search engine attempts to match our words with categories in its index or directory. When a match occurs it is called a "hit" and put on a list that appears on our monitor screen.

The second main part of a search engine is its index, sometimes called a catalog or directory. Everything the spider finds when it crawls through a site goes into its index. Think of the index as a place where a copy of every Web page found by the spider is stored. Many directories depend upon people to organize them.

The third part of a search engine is software that searches through its index or directory, finding and making what it found readable or printable. This part of the engine is its browser. It is the software that searches the index, containing hundreds of millions of pages of information that the spider collected, and selects those it believes matches the keywords entered by someone doing a search. In this book we use the most common term, "search engine," to cover all of these functions.

Types of Search Engines

There are many different kinds of search engines and most of them are very versatile. For example, almost all will let you search keywords, titles of documents, URLs, the full text of a document, or just headers. Some of the search engines do a better job for some of these kinds of searches than others. But that should not be your concern as a teacher. The best search engine for you is the one you know and like the best. This choice will emerge as you gain experience with different engines.

Tips for Internet Searching

This might seem like sacrilege in a book on using the Internet, but you often can find more authoritative information in the library than on the Web. One reason is that much of what is on the Web cannot be found by an individual search engine.

Another problem is that the Web is brimming with personal opinions and misinformation. Much of this information is not rigorously edited or reviewed before being put on a site. Print materials that appear on library shelves are customarily edited by professionals, printed by publishers intent on protecting their reputations, and selected for purchase by experienced information specialists.

Lastly, skillful Web site designers organize the information at their sites to increase the chances that a variety of search engines will find it. Thus your search engine might produce a list for you that includes sites cleverly organized so they appeal to the criteria that spiders use to evaluate the information they crawl over. If this happens, a Web site can appear near the top of your hit list, but contain irrelevant, unreliable, or highly suspect information.

Searching Strategies

1. Think about the result you want before starting an actual search. It is a good idea to write down what you want to find and then search for words and phrases from your description that refer to specific items instead of general categories. Very general keywords can produce a list of millions of sites. Some experts maintain that the best possible first search will yield no results at all. This is because you have asked your search engine to find something that is very specific. It is usually easier to enlarge the search rather than to make it smaller. Also, be sure to use different search engines. You will be surprised at the varied results you get.

2. Expect to make your search several different times in several different ways. Remember, however, to save useful results from each search. There are several ways to do this. If you are using the software called Netscape to reach the Internet, put your mouse pointer on the word "Bookmark" in the toolbar at the top of your computer screen. Click on it and a short menu of options will appear on your screen. Clicking on "Add Bookmark" will store the address of the site you are visiting in your computer. When you wish to return to this site, all you need to do is pull down the Bookmark menu again, find the site, and click. Your computer will return you to that site. If you are using Microsoft's Internet Explorer, the word is "Favorites" instead of "Bookmark." Clicking

on it will give you a menu that will allow you to add a "Favorite," or go to one you have already entered.

3. The second way to save important information is to select the text you want to save from the information on your screen. Do this by holding down the button on your mouse and scrolling over the text. When you have highlighted the text you want to save, go to *Save As* on the pull-down menu, located under *File* on the toolbar at the top of your screen. Your computer will then ask you to give your text selection a name. Give it a name, select *Save*, and you're done. You have just saved the highlighted text as a file that you can open through your word-processing software after you have left the Internet.

4. Think about different ways to find the same thing. For example, if you are looking for data on "capital punishment," you might also want to include in your search the phrase "death penalty." If you are looking for "services for child care," you might also want to include in your search phrases such as "day nurseries" that have the same or similar meaning as your original term. Use everything that you know about the subject you are searching, and pay attention to information you find that is not exactly what you are looking for. Analyze the results of your search and select new keywords that seem more likely to lead you to where you want to go.

5. Avoid the temptation to scroll. Beginning searchers are often intrigued by the fact that they have found hundreds—perhaps even hundreds of thousands—of references to their subject. Scrolling through the results, page after page, is a great waste of time, and you very rarely find what you can use. It is a much better practice, and more efficient, to narrow your search in accordance with some of the tips given above.

6. If you cannot find what you want with one search engine, try a metasearch that uses a wide variety of search engines simultaneously. One such program is Dogpile *(www.dogpile.com)*. The results of a metasearch will include lists of sites compiled by numerous search engines. The names of the search engines will appear on your screen with the number of sites each found. You will then be able to select the lists you wish to view.

7. To find out almost anything about various search engines, go to a site called Search Engine Watch, *http://searchenginewatch.com*.

8. Two of the most frequently-used ways to search the Internet are by the use of keywords and phrases. Remember to enclose phrases in quotation marks, for example "genetically modified foods." Let

us assume we are interested in finding information on genetically modified foods. These are typically foods that have been produced from seeds that are created by splicing genes from one plant onto the genes of another plant. If you simply search on the keyword "genetics" or "modified" or "food" you will get hundreds of thousands, perhaps millions, of hits. In a case like this you will want to try a phrase search. Most search engines will recognize a string of words, such as "genetically modified foods," as a valid search phrase. But even this will give you far more information than you can use. You have to make your search more specific. This is where Boolean logic comes in.

Boolean Logic

George Boole (1815–1864) was a brilliant 19th century British mathematician. By merging algebra and logic, he laid the foundation for the digital revolution that led to the computers of today.

A Boolean search is one that allows the searcher to include or exclude documents from a list of hits by means of three main operators. They are AND, NOT, and OR.

For most of the work in problem solving, a Boolean search will be quite helpful. Boolean operators impose conditions on your search. For example, let us assume you want to learn about new soybeans that have been created through genetic modification.

Using Boolean operators, you could do this search by typing: "genetically modified seeds" AND "soybeans." Boolean operators allow you to narrow your search to fewer items by putting more conditions on the search. AND does this by telling the search engine to retrieve only those documents that contain both "genetically modified seeds" and "soybeans." But suppose this list of hits is too long, including material on corn seeds as well as soybeans. What word or phrase could you add to your search, that would limit the list of materials to only those about soybeans?

AND NOT would do the job for you. AND NOT narrows the search by leaving out a subset of items. To get rid of materials about corn from your search for information about soybeans, you might search using the phrase *"genetically modified seeds" AND soybeans AND NOT corn.*

Search engines are powerful tools for Internet searching. You will get more chaff than wheat until you learn general search strategies and the rules for using your favorite search engines.

Appendix III _____

Creating Your Own Problem-Based Learning Units

Inspirations

After using one or more of the problems in this book, you might want to construct Problem-Based Learning units of your own. Designing effective units involves careful attention to four important steps.

Building a unit begins with working forward or backward from an inspiration to the construction of an ill-structured problem. To work forward, start with an objective or goal in a curriculum document and construct a problem that features the targeted objective(s). Working backward begins with finding an actual ill-structured problem in a newspaper, magazine article, previously taught unit or textbook page, or on public radio or TV. Then modify it to fit your curricular responsibility.

The object of an inspiration is to provide goals, or the actual model for a problem, that will take students to important learning outcomes through the experience of real-world problem solving.

Begin your search for an inspiration by looking for:

- Decisions to be made
- Dilemmas to be resolved
- Processes or concepts to be understood
- Controversies to be resolved
- Products to be designed (or redesigned)
- Mysteries to be explained
- Artistic productions to be created
- Problems to be solved

Inspirations for problems can be found almost anywhere, but are especially plentiful in:

- Newspaper stories
- Radio commentaries
- Literary themes and characters
- Textbook accounts
- Children's stories
- Television shows
- Journal articles
- Movie situations
- Personal experiences
- Community issues
- Previously taught units
- Magazine features

Brainstorming for Content

The purpose of Problem-Based Learning is to simultaneously develop the knowledge base and problem-solving abilities of our students. The scenario students meet at the opening of their Problem-Based Learning unit will contain an ill-structured problem. This becomes the vehicle to accomplish the learning goals mentioned above.

Before getting into the details of designing a Problem-Based Learning unit, get a sense of the content the problem will bring to your students, as well as the opportunity it will offer for problem solving. Brainstorm both of these possibilities by building a web diagram around the potential ill-structured problem your students are likely to meet, based upon your inspiration (see page 181).

To build a web diagram, start with a piece of newsprint. The example provided here is based on Problem-Based Learning Unit 6 of this book. In a circle in the middle of the paper briefly describe a problematic situation the students might meet at the opening of your unit. Then construct a number of content branches that radiate from the center circle. These branches contain concepts and information students will meet and use as they resolve their problem.

Here are a few examples of problematic situations, based upon inspirations, that might find their way into the center circle of a web diagram. With each example is a possible goal for the eventual unit.

In the following situations, the students are:

- Artists about to do a watercolor of a still life (goals: use tools and skills for producing a watercolor; experience with the artistic enterprise)

Beginning Web Diagram for the Brent Spar Inspiration

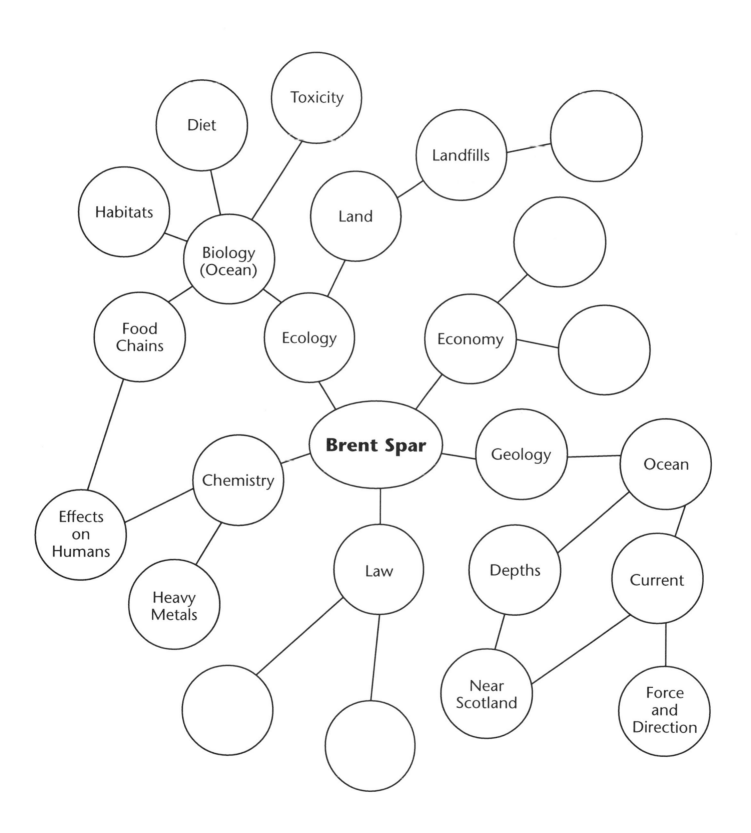

- Lawyers for a community that has received a request for a parade permit from a hate group (goals: learn how the 1st Amendment works in the real world; use of legal precedent)
- Journalists in Hiroshima in 1945, writing the first story about the effects of the atomic bomb (goals: use of the content of John Hersey's *Hiroshima* to write a news column; journalistic decision making)
- Magazine editors assigned to prepare an article for an upcoming issue (goals: learning about grammatical use; deeper understanding of the story's subject; style manuals; techniques for good writing)
- Basketball coaches who must decide which team member shoots a technical foul (goals: introduction to probability and how it works in the real world)

To construct the web diagram, put a ring of smaller circles around the center circle on your paper. In each new circle identify a concept or topic that is probably involved in the study of the situation in the center of the sheet. For example, in the Brent Spar situation (see diagram), circles are labeled ecology, economy, geology, law, and chemistry.

Around each of these circles should be placed another ring of yet smaller circles. Connect them to their host circles. As an example, around biology (ocean) you might link circles in which the ideas of food chains, habitats, diet, and toxicity are written. The process of orbiting component concepts about larger concepts continues until you are satisfied you have a snapshot of the ideas and skills. These can then be highlighted in your unit plan.

When you have completed your web diagram, look it over an ask yourself four questions:

- Is the content on this diagram significant?
- Does the content, including skills, fit my curricular responsibilities?
- Is the content appropriate for my students? (This involves the complexity of the content as well as the possibility of controversy.)
- Does it seem likely that a Problem-Based Learning unit can emerge that will fit the time I plan to use for the unit?

If you are satisfied with your answers to these questions, it is time to start crafting an opening scenario for your Problem-Based Learning unit.

Creating a Stakeholder and Situation for Your Unit

Problem-Based Learning units open with the students meeting a situation in which they have a role or stake. This opening scenario must be built carefully so that it leads students to the objectives you want to accomplish.

Opening scenarios should be engaging for the students, contain just enough information and clues to launch the process of inquiry, and provide a productive context for students as they work through the unit.

The situation your students meet should be challenging, engaging, and likely to launch their inquiry in the direction you want it to take. Look over the situations that open each of the problems in this book. What features make the situations engaging for students? What clues are provided in the text that cue students to important issues and questions that will further their understanding of the problem? What types of authority, responsibility, and power does the stakeholder's role give to the students? Why is this authority and power important for the investigation? What features in the situation seem to make this problem concrete enough to be used in the time allotted the unit?

You will need to answer the same questions about your own scenario as you design your own Problem-Based Learning units. Don't be surprised if creating an opening scenario takes some time and several rewrites. Don't be surprised either that the scenarios will be even better after they have been used with a group once, then edited.

Building the Coaching Plan

The last step in building a unit is to organize the strategies and resources you will need to coach the problem effectively. This involves completing plans for coaching students through four distinctive phases of activity during the unit. In order of their appearance, the phases are engagement, inquiry/investigation, resolution, and debriefing.

Coaches may deliver short episodes of direct instruction during the inquiry to help students with especially complex ideas or skills. Student inquiries also often involve iterations of the reasoning process, demonstrating the persistence needed during real problem solving. The inquiry phase of the unit usually concludes with formation of a problem definition or description.

Constructing the Plan

Understanding the phases used during a Problem-Based Learning unit is important for the construction of the coaching plan. The plan specifies how to make best use of the phases with the targeted learners.

The coaching plan organizes the activity during each phase of the unit. It identifies essential questions that will produce key concepts and generalizations, resources for use by students during the inquiry process, and ideas for authentic assessments.

Coaching Plan for PBL Units

Unit Title _____

Description of Action	Key Concepts, Questions, and Generalizations	Resources for Inquiry and Direct Instruction	Authentic Assessments

To develop a coaching plan, try using a form with four columns. The first column is labeled *Description of Action*. In this column the action that will take place in the classroom is described as the several sessions in the unit unfold. Also described are the types of student groupings you will use, when materials will be distributed, and when direct instruction might take place. This column will also give you an idea of just how long the unit will take to unfold. Remember, Problem-Based Learning units have yeast in them. When they get started, they are more likely to get longer than shorter.

The second column of the coaching plan is titled *Key Concepts, Questions, and Generalizations*. Its entries parallel the activities in the first. Alongside the descriptions of instructional activity, you can note important concepts and generalizations to focus on during discussion, and list essential questions you want to use with your students.

The third column lists *Resources for Inquiry and Direct Instruction*. The resources can include Internet sites and printed materials you plan to use along the way. The third column is also a good place to identify the topics for direct instruction. If you plan to use graphic organizers during discussions or to organize information from Internet searches, describe them in this column.

The last column is extremely important. As you describe the activity for each session, record ideas for *Authentic Assessments* in the fourth column. An authentic assessment has the look and substance of tasks completed by the actual stakeholder faced with the problem. For example, a professional faced with the same problem as that being worked on by the students would collect important data and organize it to assess its value and application to the problem. The problem solver would then summarize its relevance and importance to the question and issue under study if the information is to be shared with colleagues. The same would be expected from the students. Their completed organizers and summaries can then be assessed with the aid of a rubric (see page 24 for information on rubrics), describing performance standards. These standards should be consistent with those used by real problem solvers: precision of thought, persistence of effort, depth of understanding, clarity of expression, accuracy with skills and processes.

Designing your own Problem-Based Learning units might seem a little taxing to begin with, but the learning curve is fast. You should be able to find your rhythm in no time. Don't forget the following points as you work:

- Find an inspiration for your unit and use it as your model.
- Brainstorm the potential content in your inspiration before investing too much time in its development.
- Create an opening scenario for your unit with careful attention to the situation and stakeholder role the students will assume.
- Provide enough clues and cues to initiate fruitful inquiry.
- Aim for the look and feel of an authentic situation.
- Construct a coaching plan that maximizes the situation you have created.
- Tighten the length of the unit so there is little chance of wasted time.
- Break big problems into smaller problems.
- Don't try to pack everything from a traditional unit into one problem. Traditional activities can fill out a unit after the problem has been completed.

Appendix IV

Responsible Use of the Internet

The resources for problem solving that are on the Internet are mind-boggling. Even the most experienced researchers access and use only a small portion of what is available. Because the resources are available through remote access and nontraditional formats—such as computer labs, video monitors, and laptops in our own living rooms—the temptations to be lax in the ethical aspects of our behavior are strong. Students should be taught that civility and scholar's etiquette are no less appropriate on the Internet than they are in traditional libraries.

A recent poll showed that elementary and secondary teachers are enthusiastic about the Internet. Over half of them thought that children should start learning how to use it before the fourth grade. On the other hand, over half the teachers, when asked to grade themselves on their knowledge of the Internet, gave themselves a C or a D, while 19 percent gave themselves an F.

Most Internet users indicate they are aware of unethical practices taking place on the network, but fail to see the harm, unless the issue involves pornography or credit card abuse. It seems that both teachers and students need to learn how to use the Internet properly, productively, and ethically.

Not Everything Goes

What you are allowed to do on the Internet is a very complex issue influenced by the law, politics, and ethics. Teachers routinely indicate that they want to use the Internet to locate hard-to-find information and other resources. They want to use the Internet to get information on current events so they can bring their textbooks up to date.

Fortunately, the Internet is constructed to perform these functions. It is important, however, to recognize that the Internet is not watched over or managed by a legal or governmental agency. It is an open system. This means that Internet users must be very careful about how they use their freedom. Questionable uses of the Internet always bring calls for censorship and fiscal restrictions.

Every user of the Internet should always remember that somebody wrote everything on it. Often the authors have property rights to what they wrote. Every country has a somewhat different set of copyright laws. In most cases it is perfectly appropriate for a teacher to download material for use in his or her class. But it is not appropriate for a teacher to download a file, then send it out on the Internet to others, unless the author of the original material has given permission.

Property rights are especially important when using publicly available software. Sometimes hackers and other criminals put copies of commercial programs on the Internet. Even though anybody can get that software, it still must be licensed from the person who holds the copyright on it. To use it, a valid software license is necessary. As responsible users of the Internet, we must resist the temptation to help ourselves to a resource that may be available illegally or unethically.

What Is Acceptable and What Is Not

There are rules about the acceptable use of the Internet. A complete copy of these rules can be found at *http://www.merit.edu/michnet/policies/acceptable.use.policy.html*. Although this is the policy of the National Science Foundation and not the whole Internet, it is a good guide to how teachers and students should use the Internet.

- The gist of this policy is that open research and education are supported for schools and research organizations.

- The Internet is not to be used by schools and educators for any other purposes, including business or advertising. Educators are free to use it in connection with research and instruction.
- They can also use it to communicate among themselves for professional development and to debate issues related to teaching.
- They can also use it in applying for or administering grants or for contracts for research or instruction.
- They are not supposed to use it for fund-raising or public-relations activities.
- They can use it for any kind of administrative communications or activities that directly support research and instruction. For example, they can announce new products or services for use in research or instruction.
- As educators, it is not acceptable to use the Internet in order to make a profit or for private or personal business.

There are many other policy statements about the proper uses of the resources of the Internet. Many of them stress that if the resources are used irresponsibly, future support can be jeopardized. The reason is that the government sponsors of the system have a responsibility to the public to allocate government resources wisely and effectively. If disruptive abuses occur justification for the support of the system suffers. Access to the Internet is a privilege, and should be treated as such by all users of the system. Unacceptable uses of the Internet are of five general kinds.

Unacceptable Uses of the Internet

Any activity that:

1. Tries to gain access to resources on the Internet for which the user is not authorized
2. Disrupts the use of the Internet
3. Wastes the resources of people, computer capacity, and the like
4. Destroys the integrity of computer-based information
5. Compromises the privacy of the user

There are some things that are acceptable on the network but should be avoided because they are potentially politically damaging. For example, Congress and those who pay the bills take a dim view of excessive game playing. They have also attempted to pass bills to censor the Internet because of anti-social behavior that is hateful and harassing. Public opinion and political pressures have already forced the closing of at least one site that offered publicly accessible obscene files. Inflicting intentional damage, interfering with others, and making dangerous information available—bomb-making suggestions, for example—are certainly reasonable prohibitions.

Security

This list of unacceptable uses shows that all users must pay attention to the protection of the security of the Internet. Security issues are of two kinds: the security of the whole system and the security of the user's own system.

Unfortunately, an open system attracts criminals and hackers whose aim is to destroy and steal. More than once hackers have tried to destroy the system by introducing "worms."

A worm is a program or command file that uses the computer network itself to destroy its own integrity, reliability, and availability. A worm generally spreads a self-contained program to other computers over the network. It is a self-replicating program that burrows into computers that have certain loopholes in their programs. Fortunately, the Internet is protected by an association of security response centers that cooperate with each other. Most worms are eradicated before they cause insurmountable damage.

Password Security

There are several things that the individual user should do to keep the Internet secure. First, everyone should understand the security policies and procedures of his or her own computer and network site. Here are some of the things that the user should do to insure the secure operation of the Internet.

- If passwords are required, follow the procedures for protecting your password. If you need to use a password, be sure to select it carefully and change it often. Some sites have requirements about how often to change it. If they do not, it is suggested that you change your password every six months, at the minimum. Do not create a password using a word from any language or words spelled backwards. Hacker criminals have many programs that test for words like this. Construct your password using numbers and letters and keyboard symbols such as the pound sign.
- Remember that users are responsible for all the resources that are assigned to them. Do not share any computer accounts or access to resources that are assigned to you. You do not know how someone else will use those resources or give them away.

- Never leave your terminal logged in and unattended. Anybody who knows much about computers can examine any of the resources assigned to you and take or use what they want.
- Do not store your password on the computer. It makes it too easy for other people to find it. Write it down in a place other people are not likely to find.
- A password should be at least six characters long, and it should not be a set of adjacent keyboard keys. If you have trouble picking a password or remembering it, choose a song lyric or a literary phrase and use the first letters of words in a sequence. For example, "My country 'tis of thee, sweet land of liberty" would yield MCTOTSLOL.

Virus Security

Another important threat to the effective use of a network is a virus. A virus is a computer program that is designed to somehow alter or destroy a computer system. It sometimes enters the user's system by way of an infected floppy disk. Often it is hidden in a file that is downloaded from another computer through a modem.

Criminal hackers are ingenious. They have created viruses that erase data files, reformat hard disks so that all the files on the disk are lost, or just destroy your system files so that you are not able to start the machine.

Most viruses copy themselves and infect any disk in the system. To protect your system against viruses, install an anti-virus program, then keep it up to date. A good anti-virus program first checks to see if any viruses exist in your system. If they do exist, the best anti-virus programs can clean out the viruses. After that is done it can inoculate your system against any future viruses. Many systems run anti-virus programs continuously to check for incoming viruses.

Another measure you can take to protect your system is to isolate it. It is not as effective or practical as an anti-virus program. But do not let anyone put a disk into your computer without your knowledge. Neither you nor anyone else should copy files from an unknown or untrustworthy source into a computer.

Participating in News or Chat Groups

One of the most important things that teachers use the Internet for is to talk with other teachers and share curriculum ideas and teaching methods. There are many newsgroups and chat groups that serve this function. For them to function effectively, some rules need to be followed.

Shorthand When Conversing on the Internet

BTW .... "By the way"

CWYL .... "Chat with you later"

FYI .... "For your information"

GIWIST .... "Gee, I wish I had said that"

HEHEHE .... An abbreviation for laughter

IMO .... "In my opinion"

OTOH .... "On the other hand"

POV .... "Point of view"

"Smiley faces" express emotion on the Internet.
Read these characters sideways.
Using all capitals (HELLO) is considered shouting.

-) .... Happy

:-D .... Very happy

:) .... Cynical smile

: -l .... Grim

: -/ .... Very grim

: -(....................... Sad

: -\ .... Puzzled

   To interact in productive ways, it is necessary that several conventions be followed. The rules that follow aim to promote effective and efficient interchange of ideas.

   Observe first. Before you participate in a group, observe for a while. This means reading what goes on before you post a message. You will see how the users interact, the topics they cover and how you should enter the conversation. When you do enter the conversation, there are guidelines that will make your participation more effective.

   Keep it brief. If you can state your ideas briefly and concisely, they will have a greater impact. Generally speaking, the longer the message, the fewer the people that will bother to read it.

Try to make your postings easy to read and understand. They should be in good form and spelled correctly. You do not want to post something that will embarrass you later. Keep your spelling correct but do not bother to correct others.

Think about your audience before you post a message. For constructive conversation you want to reach the appropriate audience. Choose your newsgroup carefully. Some chat and newsgroups are limited in terms of the geographic area they represent. Before you post, be careful about the group you are posting to. Do not post to groups you do not read.

When you are commenting in a discussion, summarize the topic. You cannot expect the readers of your comments to remember what the original said. One way to do this is by quoting the major points from a previous remark to which you are responding.

When you answer a question that someone has asked, use email to reply. When someone asks a question the group is often flooded with people who send identical answers to it. This wastes resources and time. Answer the question with email. Perhaps the person who asked the question will have the courtesy to summarize all the answers to the group.

If you ask a question, ask people to send you the answers by email. Then you can summarize the answers and post your synthesis to the network.

Pay attention to copyrights and licenses in your postings. The law is not clear about many aspects of ownership of material posted onto a network. Many courts hold that it is in the public domain, unless certain very specific conditions are followed. The best way to protect your ideas is to copyright your posting, and put the copyright notation in the posting.

Re-posting anything published under a copyright could lead to legal problems. You and your school could be held liable for damages. Avoid plagiarism. If you are using facts to support your arguments, cite the appropriate references. State where they come from.

Proper Behavior When Using the Network

The general principles that guide good network ethics and behavior recognize that individualism is respected and encouraged, and that the network is a valuable resource that must be protected.

Whatever you put on the network anyone who has access to the network can retrieve. Be very careful about what you say about other people. It is a good rule to never post personal information about yourself or other people.

Communicating with a computer is very different from live communication. When you talk person-to-person, voice inflections, facial expressions, body language, and the like are important parts of the communication. That is not the case with print. Humor and sarcasm are to be avoided because they are easily misinterpreted.

A good general approach to using the Internet politely is to think of yourself as a guest using someone else's equipment. As you will soon find out when you use the World Wide Web, the system is heavily used and is already very slow. Do not contribute to this by prolonged sessions. Figure out what you want to say before you start to send.

Try to limit your sessions to times in the day when demand is lowest for the site you want to use. This benefits both you and others because it lessens the time you have to wait, and distributes the load on the system.

One of the great things about the Internet is its freedom from controls and allowance for individual expression. This is a two-edged sword. The danger side of the sword is that unsuitable material and misuse that could hurt the Internet. The good side of the sword is that it is a place of great freedom. When you are tempted to be offended, remember that the restrictions you might want to impose could grow and become restrictions on you. Following simple rules of good behavior will make the Internet a more effective institution for everybody.

Cheating

Many schools and colleges are having problems with student use of the Internet because of cheating. There are services on the Internet that will write papers on any topic for a fee. There is much material that is easily and quickly copied. As a result, some teachers no longer grade papers unless they can give the students a written or oral examination about the material.

A good teacher often can sense a problem when an average student turns in a superb paper. The situation is much more difficult when good students turn in copied papers. Teachers must be very careful about the assignments they give. They must teach the students to credit all the sources they use, including Internet sites, search engines, and search terms. Teachers must read student papers with a new awareness.

When students use information from Internet sources in their work, they should be able to cite their site when asked. In written work, students should be asked to provide citations just as they would if they were working with printed material from the library. A number of sites on the Internet provide excellent guidelines for citing electronic materials. *The Longman English Online Citation Guides* are available at *http://longman.awl.com/englishpages/CYBER4.HTM. The Columbia Guide to Online Style* can be found at *http://www.cas.usf.edu/english/walked/mla.html.*

Glossary of Internet Terms

Address: A unique set of letters and numbers that specifies where a person, machine, or data is located on the Internet.

Applets: Parts of special Java programs that are downloaded and run on your machine. They are an important part of the Java programming language. The Java language is one of the most powerful and popular programming languages for applications on the Internet. Some applets only harass and annoy; some are destructive. Accept Java applets only if you have proper security.

Backup: An extra copy of material that is stored apart from the original material in case it is lost or damaged. By copying the files you have saved you can restore them to the condition they were in at the time you saved them. Back up often.

Bookmarks: Sometimes called Hotlists or Favorite Places. They are lists of frequently selected Web addresses. Web browsers allow users to create bookmarks so they can return to favorite sites without much trouble.

Boolean Logic: A strategy that uses AND, OR or NOT to refine an Internet search.

Browser: Software to find and retrieve information on the Internet. Web browsers are programs that are used to access the World Wide Web and allow a person to read hypertext. The browser gives some means of viewing the contents of nodes (or pages) and of navigating from one node to another. Netscape Navigator, NCSA Mosaic, Lynx, and W3 are examples of browsers for the World Wide Web. They act as clients to remote Web servers.

Client: One usage refers to software that works to extract some service from a server. It is also often used to refer to one computer that makes requests for data from another.

Cookies: Some Internet sites set up files on your hard drive and store information in them. Cookies can keep track of when you come to the Web site, what you do when you get there and almost anything else the system designer wants to know. They can be abused. They are useful when a site is visited repeatedly, for example by saving the user time in registering. Because many people do not like their privacy invaded, software exists to foil the cookies. It either sends the cookies fake information or deletes the cookies on the hard drive.

Data: Information that is stored in a computer system. A database is a collection of information that is stored in a computer. Many can be searched by the Internet user.

Directory: A list of files.

Domain Name System: Often abbreviated as DNS. In order for the Internet to function, every machine connected to it must have a unique address. The DNS keeps track of all the names and address of all the machines on the Internet.

Download: To download refers to the transfer of a file to the user's computer from some other computer. The opposite of upload, which sends a file from the user's computer to another computer. Both downloading and uploading refer to the movement of files between computers.

Email: An abbreviation for electronic mail. A message sent from one computer to another.

Email Address: An address used to direct messages on the Internet. It is usually of the form username@hostname. "Username" stands for the computer address of the person or group sending or receiving the email. "Hostname" stands for the machine or organization through which the user sends or receives information.

File: The name under which computer programs, documents or other software applications are stored. There are two main kinds, data files and program files. Program files are those that control how the computer operates. Data files contain information of various kinds.

Gofer: A program for browsing the Internet using a menu. It allows access to Internet hosts that provide Gofer service. It is a menu-based system whose Internet function is to go for or gather information.

Homepage: This is what appears when a user accesses a World Wide Web site. It is the table of contents to that Web site.

Host: One of the individual computers that are connected to the Internet. The hostname is the name of a host that corresponds to its address. A host contains the information or service requested by the client.

http: An abbreviation for Hyper Text Transport Protocol. The set of rules which programs must follow for Web users to communicate with servers and transmit information back and forth. It allows the use of text, hypertext, graphics, video clips, and sound. As the first instruction to an address to the World Wide Web, it is always in lower case, http:/.

Hyperlink: A colored or highlighted (often underlined) word or picture on a Web page. When it is selected it takes the user to a related piece of information.

Index: The searchable catalog of documents created by search engine software. Also called catalog. Index is often used as a synonym for search engine.

Internet: A world-wide collection of computers that are interconnected in such a way that they can communicate with each other. The computers have hardware and software that provide access to the databases they contain. It is the global network of computers that includes all of those interconnected by TCP/IP networks.

Internet Service Provider: Abbreviated ISP. An organization that provides access to the Internet. A service provider sets up connections from the user to the Internet. When one purchases an Internet account, one is assigned a password and an email address as well as the number to call in order to access the Internet.

IP: An abbreviation for Internet Protocol. The systems of rules for communications that are used by computers on the Internet. It is the most important protocol for the Internet. An IP address is the unique numerical Internet protocol address assigned to every computer on the Internet.

Keyword: A word or words that are used in searching for documents or menus.

Login Name: This is the name you use to access services on your own computer. It identifies you, and only you, to the computer system. Sometimes it is also called USERNAME or USERID. To login to a computer means to sign on and activate it for use.

Menu: A list that provides information about where other information can be found.

Metasearch: A search using more than one search engine.

Modem: An acronym for Modulator/Demodulator. It is a communications device that enables a computer to transmit information over a telephone line. It is a combination of hardware and software that attaches to the computer and to a phone line or other communication medium.

Netiquette: The social rules for sending communications over the Internet. It refers to manners.

Online: It refers to the situation when a computer is connected to any carrier: the Internet, a bulletin board, an online service, or another computer using communications software. Opposed to offline when the computer user is working only with an individual computer and is not connected to another.

Operating System: The fundamental software that controls the computer. It is abbreviated OS. System software includes programs that are necessary to run a computer. The operating system provides the instructions that tell the computer how to operate.

Password: A string of letters, numbers, or other characters on your keyboard that you use when you sign on or log in to your computer. It is usually to be kept secret.

Piracy: Illegal use of a computer program. It occurs when a person copies a program without paying for it. It is a form of theft.

Posting: An individual sending an article or message to a news or user group is an example of posting. A post is an individual message.

Program: Software that controls the operation of a computer. A program is a series of instructions to the computer that tell the computer what to do. A program file is distinguished from a data file by the fact that the data file contains information and does not instruct the computer.

Push: The basic model for the Internet is for the user to click on an object for some response. Some software allows a sender to push information to a user's machine without any actions by the user. Some push software is user installed, for example, in the case where it is desirable to check on information that changes during the day.

Robot: Often abbreviated as Bot. For example, a shopping robot is a computer program that scans the Internet for the lowest prices for an item.

Search Engine: An application program that enables the examination of large databases for selected words or phrases. It is a program that allows for keyword searching of online information. There are hundreds of them of different types. Search engine is often used synonymously with spider and index, although these are separate components that work with the engine.

Site: A computer connected to the Internet. It is a host that allows remote access.

Software: A set of instructions that control the operation of a computer. These instructions are grouped together in programs.

Spider: A spider is the software that scans documents and then adds them to an index or directory by following links. The term is often used as a synonym for search engine or crawler. It also retrieves all the documents that are referenced in a given document.

TCP/IP: An abbreviation for Transmission Control Protocol/Internet Protocol. The basic rules that describe how material must be formatted so that communication can occur among different kinds of computers and operating systems.

Upload: See Download.

URL: An abbreviation for Universal Resource Locator. The address of any resource on the World Wide Web. It is a standard format which contains information about what kind of computer to be contacted, the path to access it and the method of communicating with it. It is sometimes used as a method of locating a specific resource on the Internet.

Virus: A hidden program installed on a computer in order to destroy work on the computer without warning the user. It infects the user's machine without his or her knowledge. Then it carries out commands that are not initiated by the user. Often viruses enter the user's system hidden in some other legitimate program, message, or file. A virus can enter a computer on an infected disk or through a file that is downloaded from another computer.

Web Browser: Software for accessing and navigating the World Wide Web.

Web Page: An online document that contains information accessible over the World Wide Web.

World Wide Web: Abbreviated WWW or www. A part of the Internet which can accommodate a wide range of materials. It is built on software that uses a hypertext-based system for browsing, searching, retrieving, and accessing the information on the Internet. It allows the use of text, hypertext, graphics, video clips, and sound. The WWW is not the Internet. It is part of the Internet. As the use of the World Wide Web grows, and consequently slows, some users now refer to it as the "World Wide Wait."

Bibliography

Internet Nuts and Bolts

Carroll, J., R. Broadhead, and D. Cassel. 1997. *1997 Internet Handbook: Educational Edition.* Scarborough, Ontario: Prentice Hall Canada Inc.

Godin, S. (ed.) 1998. *The America Online Insider's Guide to Finding Information Online.* Dulles, Va.: AOL Press.

Williams, B. 1995. *The Internet for Teachers.* Foster City, Calif.: IDG Books Worldwide, Inc.

Thinking Skills

Baron, J., and R. Sternberg. 1987. *Teaching Thinking Skills: Theory and Practice.* New York: W. H. Freeman and Company.

Beyer, B. K. 1991. *Teaching Thinking Skills: A Handbook for Secondary School Teachers.* Boston: Allyn and Bacon.

Clarke, J. H., and R. M. Agne. 1997. *Interdisciplinary High School Teaching.* Boston: Allyn and Bacon.

Costa, A. L. (ed.) 1991. *Developing Minds: A Resource Book for Teaching Thinking.* Alexandria, Va.: Association for Supervision and Curriculum Development.

Feldhusen, J. E. 1994. "Thinking Skills and Curriculum Development." *Comprehensive Curriculum for Gifted Learners*, pp. 301-324, edited by J. VanTassel-Baska. Boston: Allyn and Bacon.

Hersey, J. 1946. *Hiroshima.* New York: A. A. Knopf.

Hofer, C. (ed.). 1998. *A+ Yellow Pages, 7-12 edition.* El Segundo, Calif.: Classroom Connect.

Nickerson, R., D. Perkins, and E. Smith. 1985. *The Teaching of Thinking.* New York: Prentice Hall.

Paul, R., D. M. Binker, and K. Adamson. 1995. *Critical Thinking Handbook: High School.* Santa Rosa, Calif.: Foundation for Critical Thinking.

Resnick, L. B. 1987. *Education and Learning to Think.* Washington, D.C.: National Academy Press.

Problem-Based Learning

Barrows, H. S. 1985. *How to Design a Problem-Based Curriculum for the Preclinical Years.* New York: Springer Publications.

Barrows, H. S. 1992. *The Tutorial Process.* Springfield: Southern Illinois University School of Medicine.

Fogarty, R. 1997. *Problem-Based Learning and Other Curriculum Models for the Multiple Intelligences Classroom.* Arlington Heights, Ill.: IRI/Skylight.

Gallagher, S. A., B. T. Sher, W. J. Stepien, and D. Workman. 1995. "Integrating Problem-Based Learning Into The Science Classroom." *School Science and Mathematics,* 95 (3): 136-146.

Johnson, T. (producer). 1997. *Problem-Based Learning.* 2-tape video series. Alexandria, Va.: Association for Supervision and Curriculum Development.

Kendall, J. S. and R. J. Marzano. 1996. *Content Knowledge: A Compendium of Standards and Benchmarks for K-12 Education.* Aurora, Colo.: Mid-continent Regional Educational Laboratory.

Norman, G. B. and H. G. Schmidt. 1992. "The Psychological Basis of Problem-Based Learning: A Review of the Evidence." *Academic Medicine* 67 (9): 557-565.

Stepien, W. J., S. A. Gallagher, and D. Workman. 1993. "Problem-Based Learning for Traditional and Interdisciplinary Classrooms." *Journal for the Education of the Gifted.* 16 (4): 338-357.

Stepien, W. J. and S. A. Gallagher. 1997. *An ASCD Professional Development Inquiry Kit: Problem-Based Learning across the Curriculum.* Alexandria, Va.: Association for Supervision and Curriculum Development.

Stepien, W. J. and S. L. Pyke. 1997. "Designing Problem-Based Units." *Journal for the Education of the Gifted.* 20 (4): 87-93.

Alternative Assessments

Aschblacher, J. Herman, and L. Winters, 1995. *A Practical Guide to Alternative Assessments.* Alexandria, Va.: Association for Supervision and Curriculum Development.

Wiggins, G. 1996/1997. "Creating Tests Worth Taking." *Educational Leadership.* 49 (8): 26-33.

Electronic Sources

Ciolek, T. M. 1999. *Ethics and Etiquette of Internet Resources.* Retrieved September 24, 1999, from the World Wide Web: *http://www.ciolek.com/WWWVLPages/QltyPages/QltyEtiq.html*

Harris, R. 1997. *Evaluating Internet Research Sources.* Retrieved August 4, 1999, from the World Wide Web: *http://www.sccu.edu/faculty/R_Harris/evalu8it.htm*

Sullivan, D. 1999. *The Major Search Engines.* Retrieved September 23, 1999, from the World Wide Web: *http://www.searchenginewatch.com/links/majorsearchengines/The_Major_Search_Engines/index.html*

Longman Online Citation Guides. 1998. Chapter 2: "Finding Internet Sources for a Selected Discipline." Retrieved September 4, 1999, from the World Wide Web: *http://longman.awl.com/englishpages/CYBER2.HTM*

Longman Online Citation Guides. 1998. Chapter 4: "Citing Electronic Sources in APA Style." Retrieved August 4, 1999 from the World Wide Web: *http://longman.awl.com/englishpages/CYBER4.HTM*

Network Computing News. *"New Poll Asks U.S. Teachers About Internet." Retrieved November 27, 1996, from the World Wide Web: http://www.ncns.com/teach.html*

Productivity Works, Inc. 1999. *About the Productivity Works, Inc.* Retrieved September 24, 1999, from the World Wide Web: *http://www.prodworks.com/about.htm*

Walker, J. R. 1997. *The Columbia Guide To Online Style.* Retrieved September 24, 1999, from the World Wide Web: *http://www.cas.usf.edu/english/walker/mla.html*

Notes:

1. Search engine URLs can be found at *http://www.searchenginewatch.com*

2. Citations for specific Web sites listed in student problem logs are repeated in Chapter 4, starting on page 28.

3. An extensive number of Web sites regarding Problem-Based Learning can be found by searching the Internet using the term *"problem based learning."*

About the Authors

William J. Stepien taught social studies to middle- and high-school students for over twenty years. Since 1996, he has run the Consortium for Problem-Based Learning. As a private consultant, he has conducted more than one hundred workshops with school districts around the country. He serves as ASCD's national consultant in the field of Problem-Based Learning.

Dr. Peter R. Senn is a Professor Emeritus at Wright College, a private economist, and the author of numerous articles and books on economics, computers in education, and the Internet.

William C. Stepien teaches social studies at St. Charles High School in St. Charles, Illinois. He regularly leads professional development sessions on using the Internet.